SOCIOPATH

Learn How to Deal With a Sociopath

(A Real-life Nightmare and Helpful Advice for Every Person To Avoid a Psychopath)

Brady Ramirez

Published by Andrew Zen

Brady Ramirez

All Rights Reserved

Sociopath: Learn How to Deal With a Sociopath (A Real-life Nightmare and Helpful Advice for Every Person To Avoid a Psychopath)

ISBN 978-1-77485-137-1

Legal & Disclaimer

The information contained in this book is not designed to replace or take the place of any form of medicine or professional medical advice. The information in this book has been provided for educational and entertainment purposes only.

The information contained in this book has been compiled from sources deemed reliable, and it is accurate to the best of the Author's knowledge; however, the Author cannot guarantee its accuracy and validity and cannot be held liable for any errors or omissions. Changes are periodically made to this book. You must consult your doctor or get professional medical advice before using any of the suggested remedies, techniques, or information in this book.

Upon using the information contained in this book, you agree to hold harmless the Author from and against any damages, costs, and expenses, including any legal fees potentially resulting from the application of any of the information provided by this guide. This disclaimer applies to any damages or injury caused by the use and application, whether directly or indirectly, of any advice or information presented, whether for breach of contract, tort, negligence, personal injury, criminal intent, or under any other cause of action.

You agree to accept all risks of using the information presented inside this book. You need to consult a professional medical practitioner in order to ensure you are both able and healthy enough to participate in this program.

TABLE OF CONTENTS

Introduction

Ever wonder how criminally insane people end up like they do? Are they just following the flow? Is the criminally insane a result of luck and circumstance?

Criminally insane can be Ted Bundy or Jeffrey Dahmer, but those are the ones who get arrested and locked up. Some people are not caught and institutionalized. Perhaps the insane asylum was the place where criminally insane were kept in the 1970s. Today, the criminally insane can choose to live in jail or on the streets.

There are many methods to decode a person's true motives. There are many ways to identify signs of psychopathy, sociopaths, and criminally insane behavior. People with insanity and antisocial disorders are often unaware of their behavior until they are caught.

This book will expose "deadly giveaway" behaviors of criminally insane, psychopaths and sociopaths as well as the mental disordered. This book will reveal more about the secrets behind the "dead eyes" and the hidden dangers they hide.

Learn more about masks and deception. Learn about manipulation, deception and intimidation tactics, and how they could be used against your.

It may appear that some people are predestined to be criminally insane. How can we tell when someone is going downhill? What point in a person's life does it become apparent that they are exhibiting criminal behavior? It is possible to stop criminal behavior or recognize it before it becomes too late.

Chapter 1: Understanding How They Act

How They Act in General

Assessing the psychological state of mind has been the greatest issue in the current world today. People tend to have diverse personality ranging from a psychopath, sociopath, and narcissistic mindset which need to be analyzed for a better co-existence in the society. Naturally, there is no cause of such a psychological state, but there are some intrigued characters which one acquires as they grow up though some might be inherited from parents. Experts have come up with psychological checklist-revised to assess and measure the 20 personality and behavior symptoms for a better understanding of the phenomenon in society.

Initially, psychopaths are believed to be superficially charming, grandiose, and manipulative and are prone to blame others there for their actions. It is not easy to leave with such people in society, though we cannot chase them away since they may be our immediate brother or sister thus we must find a way to accommodate them. In most cases, they are prone to display callous lack of empathy with no remorse in their deeds. Understanding these people is much important than anything else. Generally, they are opportunistic, and they do not care about the consequences of their actions as long as they can achieve their goals. To mean, most of them tend to have extreme criminal behavior which may turn out to be more dangerous in society, and they cannot be accommodated due to that. Therefore, serious action has to be taken, and the need to be understood in the community is much necessary. Though there is no specific cause of psychopathy, to some extent it can be associated with genes that may be responsible for 40 to 60% of its development. Basically, it has been associated with the interaction of biological, psychological and prevailing social risk factors in the societal setting. Considering the consequences of living with such a mindset among us, we should inspect several risk factors that might lead to psychopathy and how they come about though it has a complex personality disorder that needs much attention.

Moreover, the need to know how psychopaths associate with sociopath is much important. It provides a platform for comparison and contrast thus creating a better understanding of the situation. On the contrary, sociopaths are believed to be superficial and are incapable of deep and meaningful relationships, and they tend to have a loose connection with others. In other words, they are antisocial, and the attachment created with these people is likely to fade very fast since they cannot pretend to be in such engagement. They usually prefer working alone in isolation. Nevertheless, they pose a unique personality, and in most cases, they are prone to more lies and deception where they do not value friendship and partnership in their lives. Viewing these kinds of people from other perspectives, they are selfish and lack empathy, and they do not care about what people may think about their actions.

Psychopath's behavior is not inherited; rather they are induced through socio-cultural factors such as from the environment. These kinds of behavior are natured, and the resultant output is not much fit for society. Understanding the kind of mindset poses by this personality may rescue some other people from copying the character due to its artificial cause. Unfortunately, the personality is somehow confused with charming and deceitful behaviors of such individuals which may prove to be dangerous to unpredictable prey. The risk of falling victim is very high, and one can easily confuse this kind of personality with being friendly which is not the case since they are deceitful, dangerous and do not care about friendship.

Moreover, they are impulsive and unreliable with no set goals of what they want in life. One only need to understand and take full responsibility for their action in case you have one as a friend. Though they possess some predictable emotions and behaviors that can be identified when you take a deep analysis of their actions. Sociopaths usually seem to be nervous, and to some point, they get agitated easily. These traits are prone to volatile actions fueled by anger thus leading to emotional outbursts which tend to hold them back from jobs and education. Luckily, they may form an attachment with some people, but they do not give a damn about the rules and regulations which may further lead them to impulsive crime.

Narcissist personality, on the other hand, is very complicated, despite having a strong personality, these kinds of people lack a core self. They do not believe in themselves, and they need validation from other people to stabilize their self-esteem. It is very common misconception that narcissists love themselves and they usually prefer their own company. On the contrary, they do hate themselves. Though there is this personality of being perfectionists, inflated self-flattery and arrogance portrayed by these individuals who may seem to be irritating, and they use such for cover-up of their real beings. These people are afraid of reality and cannot stand the truth of the matter, and for that, they usually tend to be more engrossed in their activities which may not make sense in some instances. These people seem to be strong on the surface, but emotionally they are dead, and they need revival.

In most cases, they do not appreciate other people's efforts towards them, and they tend to be perfectionists who believe that their work is the best and what others do is none of their business. Sadly, they cannot appreciate love geared towards them, and when such happen, they tend to alienate themselves from the giver. Narcissists usually have an inflated ego, and they are arrogant and bossy at the same time. These people are hard to deal with, and they normally tend to attract excess admiration from others and in turn, exploit and take advantage of these people's goodwill for their gain which is not acceptable. Their unlimited dreams for power, success, and brilliance crowd their personality, and they cannot think of others as their fellow human beings.

How They Act at Work

Psychopaths represent a small percentage of staff at the workplace through their presence is much essential to the organization in many ways. Unfortunately, these people are prone to enormous damage in the organization when given a senior management role. Though they are usually common at higher position roles due to their personality which is much essential to the organization's growth. Organizations that tend to scale up their operations tend to have these people in such positions to monitor and supervise the subordinate employees. Unfortunately, they are prone to lead to failure of the organization due to their actions which may attract negativity. For instance, these people are known for their bullying, stress, conflict, absenteeism, and staff turnover; reduced productivity is accompanied by lower social responsibility. When these people are in charge, the organization's ethical standard can be badly damaged, and these can lead to more loses at the end of the day. Such characteristics tend to destroy shareholders' value and future returns on equity.

Workplace psychopaths are known for their charming character towards their senior staff at workplace hierarchy which tends to earn them a favor. On the other hand, they are abusive to staff below their level, and they treat those staff with contempt and mischief. Moreover, they are good at maintaining multiple personas in the office setting by presenting each staff with version of themselves; in other words they usually create nicknames to every staff for identification among the colleagues. The organization psychopaths usually crave for good feelings of power and control over people at work. The higher positions in the organizations allow them to feed their egos by controlling a great number of people though they are not usually brilliant as they can deceive people that they have power over others.

In most cases, they bully their junior staff in the organization to camouflage their inferior capability of doing things. They intend to let people perform their duties and take credit for it at the end. In other words, they are kind of opportunistic at workplace.

Furthermore, working with sociopaths can be trickier if you do not know how to deal with them. They are unashamedly dishonest, and to some extent, they tend to possess a callous and manipulative behavior that may not be attractive at workplace. These people tend to be immune to their colleague's emotional state and usually try to get any chance of getting their ways, and they do not care about the consequences of their actions at all. Undoubtedly, the concept of morality is foreign to these people, and they can go to the extent of doing immoral things at work to gain attention and validation of their colleagues at the workplace. In most cases, they tend to be charming and hard to ignore, though their intentions are not genuine and they do not tend to please anyone unless they can benefit from you. According to clinical psychologist Martha Stout, the number of sociopaths at workplace is minimal, and they can

account for 4% of the total employs in an
organization.

Interestingly, sociopaths are recurrently successful in their life, depending on the career they chose to pursue; they often do well. The nature of their character enables them to go for what they want in life, and they repeatedly succeed in their career paths through determination and unending passion they put at work. The ruthlessness nature earns them great deals when it comes to business, and that is what sets them apart from the rest. People tend to emulate these people for protection and status quo at the workplace. Sociopaths are known for their high performance and charisma which attracts people towards them at all levels. These characters are attractive, and they know how to use them to get on their prey. One can mistake them for being caring and emphatic which they are not. They use their charm to achieve their purpose and get the credit out of it at the end. They can go to the extent of causing collateral damage to achieve their desired goals.

Narcissistic individuals are known for their counterproductive work behavior which may tend to hurt the wellbeing of an organization if not looked watched. They normally react awkwardly when their self-esteem is threatened. Narcissism has been discovered to be both personality disorder and trait which in most cases cannot be altered by the external factors. All we got to do is to understand the disorder and accommodate them at the workplace. Luckily, these people tend to perform well in interviews and receive favorable hiring ratings as compared to psychopaths and sociopaths. Though narcissist tends to create social impressions when given chance to express themselves and that is what makes them distinct from others, they usually have a nature of boasting to gain favorable impression with employers.

Moreover, their perfectionist nature makes them be good employees, bad employers since they tend to stress much on quality and the juniors may feel threatened when they are in authority. These people are hard to work with; they are prone to attract the attention of the employers by doing impressive work and always competitive in everything they do. In case there is a credit to be earned at workplace, they will do anything to get that credit despite working as a group. They like recognition and power to feed their egos, and they are always worried about success in the workplace. To employers, they are the best people to hire but the moment they realize that they are smarter than the employer is when all hell will break loose. They will do anything to make the employer regret hiring them in the first place, they destroy the company's reputation to build their own, and they do not care how long it will take to supers the employer. To fellow employees, they tend to be the best people to work with due to their competence, openness, and entertaining nature they possess and can adjust well in new environment.

How They Act in Romantic Relationships

Despite having a disordered personality, psychopaths still can have good relationships just like any other person. Though care must be taken when you intend to get into a serious relationship with these people. Due to their persistent antisocial behavior, boldness, emotional resiliency, and impaired empathy and remorse, these people are still our friends, and they may possess other desirable qualities. However, be prepared for other things in such a romantic relationship, this kind of people are involved where egotistical traits will have to dictate the relationship. Pathological lying is a norm when dating psychopaths and it becomes apparent when you start dating these people. They will tend to lie under any circumstance to conceal their behavior and to make the relationship last long without realizing their deceit. They do that to protect their behavior and to have their way in relationship which will enable them to achieve the desired goals. Unfortunately, it is very hard to realize that their lie is untrue and they will always wrap the story carefully without any detection of deceit in it at all. Also, they have a superficial charm that they skillfully use to get the attraction of their partners, when one gets used to that charm, they find it very difficult to deny the attraction, and instead they get addicted to them.

Typically, psychopaths have an extreme perception of self-worth. This quality enables them to create new relationships with ease, and they can easily approach confident professionals and still win their affection. They tend to crush people's self-esteem and render them worthless before they concur. The trait makes them have more control in relationship and people tend to let them rule in romantic relationships. Research shows that psychopaths have a gas lightening technique that they expend to erode victims' confidence before they take over.

Additionally, these people are good at studying people's behavior which they later use against them in the relationship through manipulation to get their way. Their manipulation is hard to resist, and anyone who tries to resist normally faces their wrath expressed through anger, nagging, and abuse. Ultimately, one cannot change psychopaths since their brain is wired like that and lack of guilt from their deeds will be the norm.

Comparably, sociopaths also tend to behave like psychopaths in the relationship, but they are more skilled in manipulation as compared to psychopaths. The master of the art of manipulation and one cannot detect their deceits since they are excellent observers who will always think ahead of you in the relationship. As a result of that, they possess an intuitive sense of humor and caring nature of others which they use as a highway to somebody's heart. Though they lack empathy one cannot tell true feelings, they only get into a relationship that they intend to benefit from, and if you have nothing to provide, they will not get in such engagement. Initially, they tend to have good communication with partners, and one may feel that they truly care which they do not give a damn about your feelings.

It is common for sociopaths to maintain a friendship with their exes and they will use any chance they have to destroy them. Occasionally, they will badmouth their exes in front of strangers and find excuses to turn the reason for their break in his or her favor to satisfy their ego. However, they will only keep beneficial exes around for favors such as information, status, money, and sex. That satisfaction is all they care about, and if their exes needed such favors in return, they would tend to be repulsive and boastful of their good life.

Furthermore, sociopaths view people as potential targets, rivals, or predators. All they see is long term connection which can be terminated anytime they are satisfied or fed up with you. Intimacy is not in their vocabulary, and anyone who tends to have a long term intimacy with them will tend to lose since all their interest is not on one person. In most cases, they tend to cheat a lot in relationships since they cannot get all the quality they desire in one person. Similarly, they are very impulsive, and on many occasions, they will tend to get what they want at the time they need it. Therefore, excessive use of thrill and stimulation is associated with these people in a relationship.

Dating a narcissist, on the other hand, may come with other challenges as well.

Relationship with this kind of person usually begins as a fairy tale where you will constantly receive their texts and us without knowing it, and they text you love texts "love bombing." They well emphasis on how you look and how smart you are and immediately you are prone to get involved with them. These people always think that they deserve to be with special people in their life, those who can appreciate them fully. All will be well with these people in a romantic relationship until partner does something they do not approve is when they turn away. A narcissist will do everything to make you feel good at the beginning, and after you have fallen for their trap, their focus is redirected towards their feelings. They tend to manufacture superficial connections in the relationship which habitually turns out to be fake.

Typically, narcissists love talking about their accomplishments and achievements constantly. If you cannot maintain conversation towards their achievement and accomplishments in life, the partner is prone to lose such relationship given that it is all that matters to them and not your achievements. Normally they exaggerate their achievements to gain adoration and acceptance in society if you cannot appreciate such characters in relationship you rather keep away from them by any means. By doing so, they do not have time to listen to other people's stories and worries since all they care about is their wellbeing and feelings of being superior. One can only win their affections through praise and worshiping their accomplishments which they tend to talk about to feed their low self-esteem.

Methods Used by Sociopaths

Sociopaths will always find their way in many ways, especially by issuing manipulative techniques to attack their opponents. They achieve this by minimizing the impact of their actions. They do so by claiming that their behaviors are not irresponsible as it may seem to the complainant and they term it as just a mere exaggeration. If you have to believe that, they are likely to concur and the impact will always be irrevocable. It is like accepting that they are right and you are wrong. Moreover, they are prone to give more lies to justify their behaviors which may prove to be the best attack for them. All they care about is the result, and they can employ any weapon to attain that at the end.

Sociopaths are good at reversing the blame on others, they will deny it in front of your eyes, and you will not believe it.

The denial tactic they employ "classic "who... Me?" the victim is prone to admit what they did not commit to satisfy sociopaths' ego. They will use the confrontation to fight back and concur the victim on many occasions. If you are weak, the chances of surviving under these people are very minimal at it calls for high time to quit.

Similarly, they will employ shunning, stonewalling to attack others. In an attempt to isolate your idea and continue with their own since they do not like confrontation and comparison. In the case of children, one will close his or her hear so that they cannot hear what you are saying. Same apply to grown-up where they will intentionally shun you down when you are talking juts to put their idea across. Generally, the less you minimize talking with these people, the more you become safe from their critics and tactful communication skills that they will use to attack you back. They beat you in your game, own field and own game rules they do not care.

Furthermore, they employ covert intimidation to attack their opponents and rule over them. Here, they get your weak spot and do anything to push on those weak points to intimidate their opponents. If one is weak, they stand a chance of losing and that is their joy.

Ultimately, sociopaths tend to play victim role of circumstances to gain sympathy from the general public, and anyone who does not know them well will give in to their tricks and deceit. They will evoke compassion and use it as the weak point to take advantage of the competitor or rival. Also, they will use a guilt-tripping trick to pass the blame on others who are not responsible for their irresponsible behaviors. By doing so, they can divide and rule over the others since they will earn the trust of their seniors.

Methods Used by Psychopaths.

Psychopaths are always associated with such behaviors as criminal acts which may not be true to all of them. Not all of them are criminals and am not justifying it with any evidence that is the fact. According to research, only one percent of the population meets the criteria of psychopaths, and it is very unusual to ignore these people in society. These people are high in Machiavellianism, which they use to attack people within society. The cunning and manipulative character sets them distinct from others and they know how to create a scene just as to attract attention of people. By doing so, they will always have their way to concur others. Their destructive tactics can be employed anytime to make their way and have what they intend to obtain. Since they disregard rules and moral standards set by the authority, they will break those rules and get the deal they want. Even if it means being disrespectful to people in authority, they do not care about anything.

These master manipulators are liked by people due to their charming and superficial pretense they put into use; they can convince people and have their way in a very simple manner. Most of the time, they will use the associates, colleagues or mates to attack other people and have a deal with them. The impressive skills they have when talking in public also make them distinct from the rest, and they usually take advantage of their courage and daring character to attack the victims. Moreover, they can craft a deceit and defamation tactic to create an emotional imbalance on the victims before they trigger that fear that will usually make them give in when making a deal.

Lack of empathy makes them superior over others. The feeling of guilt is completely absent in such people; all they think about is themselves and how they can satisfy their ego. In this case, they can use force to get what they want, and no one will compromise their actions. Generally, they lack social emotions, and you may wonder how they cope up with others in society. All they see is violence, and it does not occur to them that they are doing anything wrong. If for instance they steal something from you, even if you found such people red-handed they would not return it to you. Instead they will insult you and even beat the hell out of you in return. So funny one may say, but it is very sad!

These people tend to be self-centered, and the inflated sense of qualities cannot let them care about others. Anybody who is self-centered always tries to satisfy their needs before caring for others. In these situations, the psychopaths will always get everything they need from others to satisfy themselves. Even if it is a matter of getting the credit for what they never did, they will get that credit in a manipulative way.

Methods Used by Narcissists

Foremost, they use gaslighting techniques to manipulate and concur the victim. They tend to say that "that did not happen" by that, they will avoid the discussion and will try to convince the victim to their way of thinking. Remember these people claim to be the best always, and anything undermining their creativity and capability denied. They can use the words like "are you crazy" to question your sanity and validity of the information you are giving them. In the end, they will not take the information but use it against you. One is prone to fall a victim under their watch. Such tricks are used to gain recognition and accolades for their skills. One will likely fall for their trap and render them what they want when they want it with immediate effect. They distort and erode the sense of reality one has, and feeling of justification will only attract abuse and mistreatment.

By all means, the narcissists will always avoid being held accountable for their shortcomings. These people chronically are unwilling to be responsible for any bad deeds they had done, and instead, they will find a way to blame others. By doing so, they gain ground to build reputations which may later earn them new positions at work or make them superior thus setting them above you. When that happens, one will remain submissive to their mischiefs and manipulative tactics. They take a defense mechanism by using your negative behavior or attribute as the stepping stone to what they want in life. This character ultimately leads to digression and devoid of accountability.

Having a thoughtful discussion with such people is very difficult. One should have a conversational mindful when engaging with narcissists, and the usually devise a way to demean anyone who engages with them. They seem to have a super-mind which will always have ad hominem argument to disorient you off track when you tend to have a conversation with them. They do so o discredit one, make you feel vulnerable in their present thus having control over the situation they have created. One thing you must be aware of is their aggressiveness and lack of empathy. They will get what they want no matter the means and ways of attaining them, and in their view, they do not see any problem in getting what they want even if one gets hurt in the process.

They will always try to belittle your opinion in order to make a point. The narcissists will reframe you from making the point and make one look like a fool. For instance, one may say that something is making them unhappy, so they seek help. In their opinion, they will make one feel that they are the culprit of the problems and the device for one a way on how to change themselves. In many cases, they will tend to show the imperfection side, which may have led to such circumstances. The feelings one has are invalidated, and they take control of how one should lead their life henceforth.

Chapter 2: Epidemiology And Treatments For People With Psychopathic Tendencies

Little is understood about psychopathy although it is considered as the most serious of all types of personality disorders. This chapter will discuss the epidemiology as well as treatments for people who are suffering from this condition.

Epidemiology of Psychopaths

It is very difficult to tell whether a person is a psychopath or not thus the actual number of people in the United States showing tendencies of psychopathy is lacking. However, there are several studies that suggest that at least 1.2% of people in the United States suffer from potential psychopathy. This survey correlates the score of individual subjects in the survey regarding their alcohol use, violence and intelligence.

It is also important to take note that this condition is commonly observed among young male adults. This is probably attributed to the biochemical imbalance in the body which includes high testosterone and low cortisol levels in the body. They are also linked to people who have high suicide attempts, imprisonment, obsessive-compulsive disorders, drug and alcohol dependence and other personality disorder.

Most psychopaths are usually involved in heinous crimes and thus are locked up in jails and other correction facilities. In fact, 93.3% of all criminals detained in North American jails have psychopathic tendencies.

Psychopaths may only make up a few percentages in the population but they can cause a lot of havoc to public population that it is important to know information about their epidemiology as well as other things in order to understand what motivates them. That way, people will also be able know how to deal with them.

Diagnosis

Psychopathy is one of the most difficult personality disorders to diagnose. However, psychologists and psychiatrists have developed diagnostic tools in order to test whether a person is a psychopath or not. In this section, the different diagnostic tools will be discussed.

Hare Psychopathy Checklist: Psychopathy is determined based on the Hare's Psychopathy Checklist-Revised (PCL-R). This is a test that measures the behavior as well as emotional responses based on the interview of a subject suspected of psychopathy. People who are at the high end of the scale are considered psychopathic. The items in the checklist are split into two factors and these include (1) interpersonal personality traits and (2) impulsive-irresponsible behavior associated with criminality.

Psychopathic Personality Inventory: The Psychopathic Personality Inventory was developed without referring to the antisocial or criminal behaviors of the psychopath. This is a scale that was developed for non-clinical samples. This means that this test can be taken by an ordinary individual who wants to find out whether he or she has psychopathic tendencies.

Comorbidity: Most experts also measure psychopathy as comorbid with other types of personality disorders. Studied have indicated that psychopathy is positively correlated with other disorders such as narcissism, histrionic, paranoia, panic and obsessive compulsion disorder. Other conditions that are comorbid with psychopathy include attention deficit hyperactivity disorder (ADHD), conduct disorder and depression.

Sex differences: Sex difference is also used in determining whether a person is likely to be a psychopath or not. Recent studies have indicated that men are more at risk to having this disorder than women.

It is important to properly diagnose whether a person is suffering from psychopathic behavior or not and these diagnostic tools will help experts as well as individuals know how to deal and manage the condition of individuals suffering from this disorder.

Treatment and Management of Psychopathic Patients

Treating psychopathic patients is one of the most difficult things to do. In fact, many experts believe that psychopathy is untreatable and that there is little evidence of cure or any effective treatments that will revert psychopathy to normal behavior. However, there are evidences that some cases of psychopathy particularly those observed among juveniles can be treated. This section will deal with the different treatment and management practices that psychopathic patients should undergo.

Medical management: Although there is no drug that can treat the lack of empathy, most psychiatrists provide medicines to psychopaths in order to control their violence, aggression and other criminal behavior. Examples of drugs that are used to manage the aggression of psychopaths include mood-stabilizing drugs, antipsychotic and antidepressant drugs. However, all of the drugs given to treat psychopathic patients are not yet approved by the FDA.

Psychotherapy: The most conventional way in managing the signs and symptoms of psychopaths is psychotherapy but since they have the inability to empathize with other people, psychotherapy can oftentimes be a futile attempt to make any behavioral changes on people.

Rehabilitation facilities: Psychopaths pose threats to other people thus it is important that they be isolated from society in a human way as possible. There are now many rehabilitation facilities that offer families of psychopathic individuals, specific treatment so that they cannot inflict pain upon other people.

Psychopaths may be difficult people to deal with and there might be many experts who believe that psychopathy is difficult to treat but it is it is important that psychopaths should not be cast aside in society after all, there are evidences that can prove that psychopaths can still function normally in society.

Chapter 3: The Hidden Suffering

Psychopaths are characterized through features such as being highly intelligent, having superficial charm, poor judgment and a failure to learn through experience. They have no capacity for loving someone; they feel no remorse, no shame. They are impulsive, have a very high sense of self-worth, to the exclusion of others, are promiscuous, have no self-control and are manipulative pathological liars. The list goes on and, as a consequence of the stereotyping, the psychopath is seen as an inhuman person, cold and having no heart. But is it fair to say that for all psychopaths?

No. There are a lot of psychopaths who feel love for their families, their parents, their pets, but in their own way, what they cannot feel is any love or trust for anyone else in the world. And, contrary to popular belief, psychopaths do suffer when they lose a loved one, go through a divorce or are unhappy with their own deviant way of life. In fact, psychopaths can suffer for many different reasons. They have a deep desire to be looked after and to be loved but, because of their nature, it is not easy for a person to get close to a psychopath. Occasionally aware of their effect on others, psychopaths can also be genuinely sad about their inability to control their behavior and they tend to live a life that is devoid of any warm or close friendships.

Over time, psychopaths have been characterized as having no parental attention as a child, no guidance, a bad family life, and substance abuse by the parents as well as antisocial behavior. They are unable to sustain a meaningful relationship, and come from a background of divorce and poor neighborhoods. A psychopath may feel as though they are victims, prisoners of the fate lie has dealt them and they may even believe that they have no opportunities or advantages in life like other people.

Despite the fact that they display an arrogant attitude, there are psychopaths who feel that they are inferior and suffer from the stigmatism their own behavior calls on them. Some will adapt, albeit superficially, to the environment they live in and may even become popular people but they must work hard to hide their true natures – it simply wouldn't be acceptable to other people. This leaves them with a difficult choice in life – adapt and live a life that is empty and not real or don't adapt and live a life that is lonely and isolated.

As a psychopath gets older, he or she is unable to continue with the energetic lifestyle they have and usually end up depressed and burned out. Their health will get worse as the effects of their life comes crashing down on them.

Emotional Pain – Does it Equal Violence?

If a psychopath feels isolated socially, lonely and is in emotional pain that they associate with that isolation and loneliness, they may turn to violent crime. They will have convinced themselves that it is they against the world and will eventually convince themselves that they have the right to satisfy whatever their desires are, that they are owed special privileges. Two of the most violent psychopathic serial killers ever to have walked the earth are Dennis Nilsen and Jeffrey Dahmer, both of who said that a psychopath, a violent one, will reach a point where there is no return, where they have sliced through the last connection they had with the normal world. Because of that, their suffering, their inner sadness increases and their crimes escalate and become more bizarre in nature.

Both Dahmer and Nilsen said that the reason they killed was for company; neither had any friends only made social contact when they visited a homosexual bar. Denis Nilsen would watch the television and talk for hours on end with the bodies of his victims while Dahmer ate parts of his victims' bodies as a way of becoming part of them- it was his belief that his victims lived for longer, in his body.

For the rest of us, it is hard to imagine these people being so lonely yet both described their social failures and their loneliness as being incredibly painful and, in each case, they created their own sadistic lifestyle, their own universe if you like, in order to avenge their feelings and experiences of humiliation, abuse, neglect, rejection and emotional suffering.

Both claimed that they did not actually enjoy the killing. Jeffrey Dahmer would inject acid into the brains of his victims after feeding them sleeping pills. He wanted to control them but when he failed to do so he killed them. Nilsen simply said he felt far more comfortable with a dead body then with a live person because, he said, dead people couldn't leave him.

The reason I talk at length about these two is to highlight that, although we, rightfully, see them as cold-blooded killers, there is perhaps another side to the coin, the side we never see before it's too late.

Chapter 4: Narcissist, Psychopath Or Sociopath? Who Is Who?

NARCISSIST

A narcissist is someone who needs compassion, is gaudy and entitled. This individual is looking for approval and is presumptuous. We may guarantee that narcissism is a problem of confidence. They have immense issues with adjusting their confidence. You really can train them to be sympathetic for a moment however it isn't dependable.

At the point when a narcissist does an awful thing they feel remorseful and despicable. There is more disgrace than blame in them since they are more worried about how others see them. Their public picture is the main thing than others. For example they may feel somewhat terrible in the event that they undermine their significant other. They can think "gracious, I shouldn't have done that however I am OK so she should be OK".

Insane person

Maniac is an alternate individual. He has no sentiments of blame nor disgrace. He doesn't feel any regret when he accomplished something terrible. He couldn't care less who gets injured. That is the reason a mental case is an incredible chronic executioner or recruited professional killer. He just proceeds to do his ridiculous work. Subsequently, he returns home to have supper and sit in front of the TV with their families as nothing occurred.

The distinction between the maniac and the sociopath confound numerous individuals. A sociopath is significantly more like the maniac: he likewise does terrible things and he couldn't care less. The primary contrast is that mental case is conceived and a sociopath must prepared previously.

Insane person has an alternate autonomic sensory system. Our autonomic sensory system is that part that holds our thoughtful sensory system. Which is our battle or flight framework. Our autonomic sensory system for an ordinary individual gets energized on the off chance that we disrupt a norm. It can happen when we accomplished something humiliating or inconsiderate. At that point we can perspire, our eyes are all the way open, we glance around on the grounds that we fear results. Typical individuals don't care for those emotions.

A mental case couldn't care less as he doesn't feel by any means. That is the reason they can lie on lie indicator tests and they pull off it with no pressure. For example, he could move a dead body in his trunk and he wouldn't get restless by any means. On the off chance that the police stop him, he is enchanting and loose as he couldn't care less what is in his vehicle.

There have been doing intriguing examination with position emanation tomography(PET) checks. Where you can perceive how the cerebrum capacities. The segment of sociopath's cerebrum where is sympathy doesn't illuminate. It is latent contrasting with an ordinary individual.

A great deal of sociopaths who carry out savage wrongdoings end up in prison. The individuals who carry out middle class wrongdoings, they end up as multi-tycoons. It can occur as they can do harsh stuff in their business and traverse calm. They can require the killings for others and return to their organizations.

SOCIOPATH

Sociopath will in general have father who have heaps of solitary propensities. He learned numerous sociopathic characteristics however numerous things are hereditary and it is difficult to identify it. He will in general be exceptionally canny with shallow appeal and talkative. A sociopath is for example a child experiences childhood in a harsh area and learns guiltiness or how to be a harasser. However, it isn't generally agreeable for them. He should learn it to endure a damaging climate. That preparation may occur inside the family or inside their work. It likewise occurs in a military preparing as well.

His dad can show them how to disrupt the norms. He doesn't like this job however he must choose the option to learn it. He should figure out how to stifle their emotions and reactions to conform to another world request.

Others may state: "gracious, this is an incredible child until he got to secondary school as he got in with some unacceptable children". They learn legitimate practices to absorb into society. However, this is just a beguiling, counterfeit veneer.

Mental case and sociopath don't come in for treatment as they don't perceive any advantage to it. The main opportunity when they go to the treatment is on the off chance that they were court-requested. In the event that they end up in prison, they are upset about it.

They act first and think later. That is the reason they tend to lie, cheat, take. They will in general have conflicting work accounts since they can't hold their positions.
In the event that you engage in a

sentimental relationship with them, you are in harm's way. They like harming individuals as it gives them some delight, force, and power over them. They don't feel sympathy yet they comprehend human practices well overall. They read individuals like a book so they discover their weaknesses to utilize it against them.

Mental case, sociopath and narcissists are extraordinary chameleons. They are extraordinary controllers to change the circumstance so as to get what they need. They see the world as an instrument to satisfy their longings. Others aren't anything more like items to utilize, abuse, rebuff and obliterate.

Sociopath or Narcissist?

In case you're in a damaging relationship, you may contemplate whether your accomplice is a narcissist or sociopath and whether the relationship will improve. Assuming this is the case, or in the event that you as of late cut off such an association, it can subvert your confidence and capacity to confide in yourself as well as other people.

The marks sociopath and maniac have frequently been utilized conversely; be that as it may, sociopathy is effectively alluded to "Against Social Personality Disorder." (APD) Unlike mind-set issues, which vary, character problems, including APD and Narcissistic Personality Disorder (NPD), are suffering, unavoidable - influencing a wide scope of circumstances, and are hard to treat. Signs might be clear by youthfulness, yet a conclusion isn't

made   until   adulthood.
Determination of Anti-Social Personality

Disorder

To meet all requirements for a finding of APD, the patient more likely than not had a lead problem by 15 years of age, and show in any event four of these qualities:

Doesn't support reliable work (or school)
Doesn't adjust to accepted practices, including unlawful conduct whether captured
Dismisses reality, demonstrated by continued lying, conning, utilizing nom de plumes, not paying obligations
Hasty or neglects to prepare; moves around without an objective
Bad tempered and forceful; e.g., battles or attacks
Foolishly ignores security of self or others

Reliably reckless, as demonstrated by rehashed inability to support steady work conduct or honor money related commitments

Needs regret, and feels advocated in having harmed, abused, or taken from another

Doesn't support monogamy for over one year

Flippant and careless as a parent

Sorts of Narcissists - Malignant and Closet Narcissist A few narcissists can look like sociopaths, yet there are narcissists who aren't vindictive and who care about their families. The individuals who have all or the greater part of the 9 models for an analysis of NPD (just five are fundamental), and who show them strongly or potentially as often as possible, are viewed as threatening narcissists. They're more exploitative, awful, and ruinous.

There are a few sorts of narcissists - going from the regular "Maverick Narcissist" to the repressed or "Wardrobe Narcissist," instituted by psychoanalyst James

Masterson. They may have a mediocre mental self portrait and show proof of misery and vacancy, which the big cheese narcissist likewise has yet covers up, (additionally from oneself). Instead of look for consideration, the wardrobe narcissist may avoid it and even act humble. Like mutually dependent people, they are elevated through the romanticizing of others. As opposed to some mainstream views, this doesn't make mutually dependent people wardrobe narcissists. The last actually need genuine sympathy and have faith in their uncommonness and feeling of qualification, even in their suffering.

Contrasting Sociopaths and Narcissists

The two sociopaths and threatening narcissists can be enchanting, astute, tempting, and fruitful. They share comparative qualities of being untrustworthy, egotistical, deceptive, unscrupulous, and requiring control. Both dangerous narcissists and individuals with APD have an expanded perspective on themselves and feeling of privilege. In any event, when they're oppressive, they accept they're advocated and reject obligation for their conduct. They need knowledge, compassion, and enthusiastic responsiveness.

In spite of the fact that they may fake suitable enthusiastic responses, this is an educated conduct and not genuinely felt. Narcissists who have less and less extreme indications, alongside "narcissistic" individuals who don't have out and out NPD, can have understanding, blame, regret, and a capacity to genuinely associate, just as adoration.

Contrasts among Sociopaths and Narcissists

While sociopaths qualify as narcissists, not all narcissists are sociopaths. What drives them contrasts. In any case, the primary qualification is that a sociopath is more sly and manipulative, in light of the fact that their personality isn't generally in question. Truth be told, they don't have any genuine character. They're a definitive extortionists and can take on any persona that suits them. In this way, they might be more earnestly to spot, since they're doing whatever it takes not to dazzle you or win your endorsement - except if it serves their plan. Rather than boasting, their discussion may fixate on you as opposed to on themselves, and they can even act naturally destroying and contrite on the off chance that it serves their objective.

Like planned executioners, a sociopath is additionally computing and may plot and plan an assault a very long time ahead of time; while, a narcissist is bound to respond sooner, utilizing terrorizing and lies. Sociopaths are lazier and attempt to cheat, take, or adventure others monetarily, while numerous narcissists however exploitative, strive to accomplish their points or flawlessness. Albeit the two characters might be persuaded to succeed at all costs, narcissists are more keen on what you consider them. They need others' profound respect. This makes them subordinate and mutually dependent on others, and really equipped for being controlled. They're less inclined to separate from their mate than a sociopath, who may leave or evaporate on the off chance that they're uncovered or don't get what they need.

Help and Treatment

Individuals with NPD or APD don't normally look for treatment, except if, on account of NPD, they're encountering serious pressure, melancholy, or their accomplice demands. Those with APD are once in a while reluctantly court-requested to treatment, which in itself turns into an obstacle to defeat regarding trust and receptivity. Treatment should zero in on helping them access their sentiments and gain from the negative results of their conduct.

Numerous narcissists can improve with treatment, and the individuals who have understanding can profit by psychodynamic psychotherapy. On the off chance that you speculate you're involved with a narcissist, study and get an agenda of narcissistic practices.

Everybody is remarkable, and individuals don't generally fit perfectly into characterized classifications. Serious NPD looks like APD, and any distinctions are truly immaterial. Try not to be worried about diagnosing; all things being equal, placed your energy into mending yourself from injury or PTSD and codependency. In case you're in an oppressive relationship, look for help right away. Neither staying nor leaving is simple. Zero in on picking up mindfulness, securing yourself, and finding support and backing.

Chapter 5: Female Psychopaths

"I don't really like you, but I'm so good at acting as if I do that it's basically the same thing."

— Lisa Scottoline, Every Fifteen Minutes

While most psychopaths are male, it's possible for women to have this disorder too. Much like men, female psychopaths are born with a reduced ability to feel and empathize. A female psychopath can be as dangerous and toxic as her male counterpart. She might be your coworker, a neighbor, or even a family member. In this chapter, we'll review female psychopathy and delve further into the behavior of women with this disorder.

How to Spot a Female Psychopath?

Unlike men, psychopathic women often show through their masks. Initially, they might act as a helpless victim or a generous friend, neighbor, wife, or a loving mother. However, when provoked, she will reveal her true nature. There are times when she will act on like to her character, belittling and berating others when she feels like no one will notice.

Two-faced

If you encounter this woman, she's acting nicely with you because she's gaining something. However, if you see her get into a conflict with someone else, you will notice how aggressive and unstable she can be. The sudden mood swings can be easily noticed if you look carefully.

A fierce competitor

When a female psychopath feels threatened, she will direct aggression towards her rivals. This can be both at work and in relationships. If a female psychopath is jealous, she will target the woman who she feels is threatening her. This will go beyond common jealousy. She will get involved in this person's life and use threats and emotional blows to drive them away.

Stalking and bullying

Female psychopaths are prone to stalking, cyberbullying, and verbal aggression. They are also easily triggered into rage. You might notice a friendly-looking woman become- infuriated at little things, like getting a wrong drink from a waiter or having to wait in line for too long.

Warning Signs of Female Psychopaths

Identifying female psychopaths is a bit harder than identifying male psychopaths. This is because female psychopaths start a relationship by acting kind and submissive. They want a man to feel protective of them. They are also less prone to aggressive behaviors. While a female psychopath is not a risk for your safety, she's a risk for your mental health. She has the same lack of empathy as her male counterpart.

They make you feel guilty

Female psychopaths will prey less on your fear and more on your guilty conscience in order to manipulate. All psychopaths tend to go through life by using the path of least resistance and obstacles. However, men and women tend to do this in different ways. Male psychopaths understand that they can use their strength to dominate. Female psychopaths know that they can use their fragility to make people feel sorry and protective of them. While acting as a gentle lady, she will feel superior behind your back.

Overly pleasing

A female psychopath can destroy a person's life the same way a male psychopath can. Female psychopaths use love bombing to target their victims. They use declarations of permanent love, compliments, praise and sexual gratification to lure their victims. This can happen both online and in real life.

However, just because a woman is acting this way, it doesn't necessarily mean that she is a psychopath. Women with low self-esteem and extremely codependent tendencies can also act this way. A female psychopath gradually starts to establish control over the relationship and her partner's life. Initially, love bombing serves to convince her partner that she's fully there for him. Much like male psychopaths prey on women's innate fragility, the female ones prey on the protective nature

typical for men, and their masculine
vulnerability.

What is the 'Love Bombing' stage?

Female psychopaths, much like men, use love bombing to seduce their victims. They start their grooming intentionally and patiently. They appear trustworthy and generous, only to start using their victims in all senses of the word later on in the relationship. Love bombing serves to enforce an unrealistic image and beliefs about an ideal romance. It lures their victims into trusting these women and being loyal to them without much proof of their own involvement and loyalty. This forms an emotional dependence.

As female psychopaths start to show their real face, their partners find themselves in disbelief that the picture that they have created for themselves is false. A fabricated identity is too real in their mind to be seen as a farce. A female psychopath will go to great lengths to mimic her target's interests, goals, and values. Since women tend to be more visual in nature, she will carve herself after an ideal of a partner that her target wants and she will completely alter her way of talking, clothing, her hairstyle and even her way of walking, in order to emulate that image.

The reason why it's so hard to resist the love-bombing of a female psychopath is that she's good at preying on typical male insecurities. Men tend to strive to look dominant in women's eyes and for women to respect them. At the same time, many men are insecure about their masculinity, and it is easy to notice. This is why flattery is so successful.

Another way in which female psychopaths manipulate is that they declare love before any proof of love was shown. It could happen after only a couple of days before the couple had any time to bond or get to know each other. She will find ways to ensure her victim that they are the most important person in the entire world. Slowing down the pace of a relationship is the best way to defend yourself from a female psychopath.

When she realizes that her partner isn't easily manipulated, she will lose her interest. Maintaining your relationships, goals, interests, activities, and particularly boundaries will show the psychopath that you are not her ideal target. It's typical for female psychopaths to lose interest in men who can't be manipulated and who won't submit to her will.

Differences between Male and Female Psychopaths

Both male and female psychopaths share similar character traits. However, they display these features differently. Here's how female psychopaths act differently compared to the male:

1. Submissive

While all psychopaths are highly narcissistic, female psychopaths are less domineering in their appearance. They are more likely to show their tendencies further on into a relationship.

2. Passive-aggressive

While they may feel like they are better than you, they will still praise you. They will pretend to like you, but gossip behind your back. Female psychopaths are also different in ways in which they display aggression. While male psychopaths show their aggression actively through aggressive and violent behaviors, female psychopaths are usually more prone to passive aggression.

3. Dramatic

Female psychopaths love drama. They enjoy picking fights over small things and then causing their partner to feel guilty and inadequate. While there are more male than female psychopaths (93% of psychopaths are male), there are also women who can be both psychopathic and criminal. Female psychopaths rely more on their looks, seduction, and sex to lure victims in and manipulate them. They will use sex to get what they want. One of the strategies they use is to deny sex when something is not according to their will. In addition, female psychopaths tend to suffer more from anxiety and emotional problems and are more promiscuous.

4. Always a victim

They are little likely to confront you directly. Instead, they tend to spread gossip or make up lies. They are also skillful in gaslighting so that you question your own behaviors and even your sanity. Female psychopaths are a lot more skilled in emotional manipulation. Unlike male psychopaths, they will wait until further into a relationship to start dominating. They might even act in a submissive way, but manipulate their partners or friends through the attitude of a victim. In a fight, a female psychopath is less likely to threaten to hurt you. Instead, she will threaten to hurt herself.

Female Psychopaths and Relationships: Who They Target and How It Ends?

After the initial love bombing, a female psychopath becomes unstable, both emotionally and mentally. She acts highly emotional. However, under the surface, she's completely detached from others and uncaring. While her words are emotional, her actions are completely cold and neglectful. For example, she might lure a man into having a child with her by talking about her love for children. But when she has children, she will become completely uninterested. Here's what you can expect from a relationship with a female psychopath:

1. Control

A female psychopath will want to be in control of all aspects of her partner's life. She'll watch where they're going, go through their belongings regularly, and demand that they report on all activities. She might do this in a seemingly benign way, by acting concerned, or saying she doesn't like being away from their spouse. Either way, the purpose of this behavior is making sure no one and nothing compromises her dominance over the partner. She's ensuring no one is talking against her and working against any relationship of her partner's that goes against her interest.

2. Money loss

Female psychopaths tend to be even more parasitic than males. She'll want complete control over the victim's money, and won't be a stranger to debt. She'll treat herself with luxuries regardless of the financial capacity and manipulate her victim into getting loans and selling their belongings to please her. She'll make up devious lies and schemes to obtain money. For example, she'll fake illnesses to get the money for expensive treatments, or fabricate business investments to borrow money, only to hide it away or squander it on travel and luxuries.

3. Drama and threats of suicide

A female psychopath will cause a lot of drama in the personal lives of those around her. Whether a partner of a friend, she'll act carelessly and irresponsibly and then blame others for the consequences of her actions. When confronted about her behavior, she will resort to playing a victim and even threaten suicide to deflect the victim.

Chapter 6: How Is Aspd Diagnosed?

When there is a good reason to believe that someone has ASPD, doctors will conduct a series of medical tests and psychological exams. Such tests will help identify a diagnosis.

Physical Exam for ASPD
A series of physical exams will help to rule out other problems. Symptoms of sociopathy may mimic those of other personality disorders or mental illnesses. But, with the help of thorough physical examinations, related complications can be determined.

Doctors will run laboratory tests that may include a CBC, or complete blood count. They will also conduct alcohol and drug screening that may relate to other symptoms of ASPD. A thyroid check will also be conducted.

Psychological   Evaluation
It is also imperative that doctors run a psychological evaluation of the patient. Experts will work on exploring the behavior patterns, relationships, thoughts, feelings, and family history of the patient. Psychological tests will also include an assessment of the patient's personality.

In the process of evaluation, the doctor will ask about the patient's symptoms, including when the patient started feeling them and how severe they actually are. The doctor will also ask about how such symptoms have affected the patient's daily life, as well as if such symptoms or similar experiences have occurred in the past. At this point, the doctor will also find out about the patient's thoughts on suicide and self injury as well as whether or not the patient has a tendency of inflicting harm on others.

During the examination, the doctor will also keep in mind that an individual who is believed to have antisocial personality disorder is less likely to offer an accurate account of his or her experiences relating to the signs and symptoms of ASPD. This is why the help of family and friends in determining a diagnosis is also crucial and necessary.

It can prove to be quite a challenge to rule out antisocial personality disorder. This is due to the fact that symptoms often overlap with those of other personality disorders. But, one of the most crucial factors of ASPD is the way patients relate to other people.

For someone with ASPD, a feeling of superiority is predominant. While this person may be able to vaguely understand the feelings of others, he will show no regard for such feelings. He has very little awareness of the reality of human emotions. This is why a sociopath finds it easy to make others miserable without feeling guilty about his actions.

The American Psychiatric Association lists the criteria cited in the Diagnostic and Statistical Manual of Mental Disorders (DSM) in the diagnosis of antisocial personality disorder. This is what is used by mental health practitioners and providers as a reference for diagnosis.

For a patient to be declared as suffering from antisocial personality disorder, the following criteria must be met.

•Aged at least 18 years old
•Showing symptoms relating to conduct disorder before the age of 15; such symptoms may include the following: vandalism, stealing, bullying and animal cruelty
•Conning and repeated lying

- Repeated troubles with the law
- Aggressiveness and irritability
- Repeated engagement in assaults and physical fights
- Attempts of justifying behavior after inflicting harm on others
- Feeling no remorse or guilt after harm is done
- Showing no regard for one's safety or that of others
- No sense of planning ahead
- Acting out of impulse with no regard for consequences
- Being irresponsible
- Inability or unwillingness to fulfill financial and work obligations

Treatment for antisocial personality disorder is not a simple matter. In fact, patients often resist treatment. They are under the impression that they do not need any. They are under the impression that there is nothing wrong with them. But, the truth is, individuals with ASPD are in great need of treatment. Follow up treatments over the long term are also necessary.

In addition to specific treatments for ASPD, patients also require treatments for other conditions, which may include substance use, anxiety, and depression. In the case of ASPD treatment, both mental health and medical providers can prove helpful.

A combination of treatments may be necessary. In addition, there is no particularly set treatment for all cases. A combination of treatments that may work for one patient may not necessarily be the best one for another. In other words, the treatment shall be identified based on what is suitable for the patient's situation. The severity of symptoms must also be considered.

Psychotherapy

Also known as talk therapy, psychotherapy may be used in treating antisocial personality disorder. It can be administered as either an individual or group therapy. Sessions may also be adjusted in order to include the patient's family and friends.

While it may prove helpful in some cases, this therapy may be ineffective in others. In cases where symptoms are severe or when the patient cannot admit or acknowledge the disorder, psychotherapy may provide little or no help at all. The patient's refusal to admit the condition further contributes to the problem.

Medications

The Food and Drug Administration does not provide any specific medication for the treatment of antisocial personality disorder. But, there are psychiatric medications that may prove useful in treating the disorder. Most of these medications are used primarily for the treatment of conditions related to ASPD, including aggression. Such medications include antidepressants, antipsychotics, and mood stabilizers. Precaution, however, must be practiced in their prescription and use. These medications are at risk of being misused and abused by patients.

What's needed from family members? It is not just crucial for people with antisocial personality disorder to get professional help. Help is also critical for the family members and loved ones. There are skills that need to be learned, specifically on how to protect oneself from possible violence, anger, and aggression from the patient as well as with setting boundaries. Patients are not the only ones who need help coping. Loved ones also need to learn strategies for coping with the situation.

There are support groups dedicated to the family, friends, and loved ones of those with antisocial personality disorder. Such groups can be taken advantage of.

Is it possible to prevent the development of antisocial personality disorder? Whether or not it is possible to prevent antisocial personality disorder is uncertain. But, since there is a good way of determining the individuals who are most at risk, including neglected and abused children, there is a good chance that early intervention can help. In fact, early treatment is critical. It is also important that such treatment be administered over the long term. This approach may help prevent the symptoms of ASPD from getting worse.

The source of ASPD is believed to be rooted in childhood. In this case, the roles of parents, pediatricians, and teachers are crucial in identifying the early warning signs. Proper diagnosis may not be possible until the patient reaches 18. However, symptoms can start to show before the child even reaches 15. Behavioral signs that show violent and aggressive tendencies towards oneself and other people must be addressed as soon as possible.

When a child often comes into conflict with family members, peers, and other authority figures, when the child bullies or steals, or when the child is cruel to others and to animals, it may be a cry for help. When a child shows the warnings signs, appropriate discipline must be enforced. The child must learn proper behavioral skills. Psychotherapy and family therapy may also help reduce the chances of ASPD before it is too late.

Chapter 7: Living With A Sociopath And Being A Sociopath

Realising that the person you love, or that a close family member is actually a sociopath is a daunting proposition. It will be made worse by the fact that the person involved will not know they are a sociopath and it is highly likely that the rest of your family are not aware of this fact. Sociopaths are also very good at appearing to be charming, friendly, lovable and are often seen as the centre of attention. This will make it exceptionally difficult for you to convince anyone else who already knows them well to believe you. If you attempt to push your reasoning on others it may well be you that is labelled as having a mental disorder, or at the least that you are jealous of your sibling or lover.

It can be very hard to discover that you know the truth about someone's condition but are unable to do anything about it. Especially as you will start to become more aware of the way they manipulate those around them. Many of the options dealt with in the last chapter may not be open to you will be in regular contact with them and they already know all about you. It may be possible for you to break off all contact and start afresh in your own; however, this can be a difficult choice because it will probably involve leaving family members behind as well as the sociopath.

There are several options which can help you to live with a sociopath without them manipulating or taking over your life:

Professional Help

If you are unable to obtain professional help for the person suffering with sociopathy then it is still possible for you to seek professional help yourself. This will provide an outlet for your frustrations and your concerns; you may even gain some useful advice on how to deal with them on a daily basis.

Help does not need to be in the form of a medical professional, having a good support group of friends may be enough for you to vent your frustrations and talk tactics. The main purpose of this help is to ensure you do not become stressed or ill because of the worry and constant awareness of the sociopath's ulterior motives.

The level of help required will be dependent upon the level of involvement you have with the sociopath. If they are a family member it may be possible to limit the time you spend with them, if they are a partner then this could be more difficult and the support network will be essential.

Blame

Many people who live with a sociopath
may have done so for years before they
realise they have been manipulated and
misguided. One of the first feelings that
many of these people have when they
discover they have been manipulated is
guilt. It is natural to blame yourself for
your behaviour and the hurt you may have
caused others. However, it is very
important to understand that you were
manipulated by an expert. They know how
to play on your strengths and weaknesses
and do so to ensure the right outcome for
their needs and desires. In effect they will
have created an alternate reality for you
which you believed and influenced your
decisions. This belief was not a result of a
weak mind, it was a result of the love you
had and probably still have for a person.

Stage one in living with a sociopath, if you
choose to stay with them; is accepting that

you cannot change what has happened and that it was not your fault. You are, however, now aware of it and will ensure they are unable to manipulate you again in the future.

Reform

It is very difficult to reform someone who has no empathy for others and no feelings regarding the emotional and physical damage they do to other people along the way. This is something that is not possible without extensive professional help; it is not something you should attempt at home by yourself. The more likely outcome is that you will simply give them more ammunition to use against you. Treating these types of conditions must only be done in conjunction with medical professionals.

Devise a Plan

One of the best ways to stay sane and avoid the negative connotations of a sociopath is to devise a plan. Your plan should involve your aims and goals with accurate timelines and how you intend to achieve them. This plan should be looked at almost every day to remind you of where you are going and how you are getting there. The plan should never be shared with your sociopath.

The plan will give you something to focus on and this will help you to stay strong when dealing with the sociopath in your life. Repeating your aim in your head when talking with them will also ensure you are able to say no to them if their requests do not fit in with the plan you have drawn up. If you say no enough times the sociopath will get fed up and find someone who is more willing to do their bidding and easier to use. If this leads them into ending the relationship then at least it will not be you that is to blame. If they choose to stay in the relationship you will have a better understanding of each other, although you will always have to remain on guard concerning his personality and attempts to manipulate you.

Focus

One of the favourite tricks that a sociopath employs is to use lots of hand gestures and even to touch you often. These are all part of the way they gain power over you. They are distraction techniques and are employed to confuse you and ensure you are not aware of what they are really talking about or that they are contradicting themselves. The point of these distractions is to gain your confidence and have you believe that they have told you something secret and confidential. In return you will feel obliged to share something about yourself and this is where their power comes from. Everything they do is a game; a game that they must win at all costs and that you probably do not even know you are playing.

Professionals and others who have experienced living with a sociopath will tell you that the only solution is to leave them. This may be true, but it is often harder to do than it may appear. Firstly you will need somewhere else to go and you will need funds or a job to get started again. You will also need to consider children if you have any. Secondly you will need to be prepared emotionally not only for the wrench of separation but for their attempts to get you back. Living with anyone, even a sociopath becomes comfortable and reassuring in its own way. Separating yourself from this is not an easy decision as you will be facing the unknown. Alongside this the sociopath you are trying to escape from will use emotional blackmail and other techniques to try and stop you from leaving; another way of showing their power over you. Being a human with emotions and empathy it is surprising how many times you will go back with them!

Being a Sociopath

To fully understand the reasons why you need to leave a sociopath it may be necessary to understand what it is like to live life as a sociopath:

The sociopath is devoid of morals, or you may prefer to say is lacking a conscience, however, they are not usually naive enough to not understand that they are different to the vast majority of people.

Initially a sociopath will have problems with authority figures, they will be happy to commit crime or other morally ambiguous activities without fear of reprisal. The reason they can do this is because they believe they are better than everyone else and can do whatever they like. At this point a sociopath can sound incredibly similar to a narcissist; someone who has a love of themselves above all else. However, a true sociopath is defined by a lack of remorse or guilt for their actions. It is this characteristic which makes them most dangerous as they are able to undertake any task, no matter how horrid. They will complete it if they believe it is essential to their progress. Progress to a sociopath is simply the display of power over others; the more people they control the more powerful they feel; many cult leaders have been diagnosed as sociopaths due to this affinity with power and the ability to control others.

Being aware that they are different actually allows them to exploit others and what they perceive as weaknesses, a sociopath will not react in certain situations as a non sociopath would. They usually have no fear and will simply see the challenge, not the consequences.

Living as a sociopath means that everyone in your life is an object; your aim would be to have power over them, to control them and use them to do your bidding. Often this revolves around making life easier for the sociopath. You would not be able to form any meaningful long term relationship as you do not have the emotional capability of non-sociopaths, however, you would still not want anyone to leave your circle as this is an affront to your power. It is for this reason that you would manipulate others and emotionally blackmail them to ensure you retain that power. In effect you win the game. When people are no longer of any use they are simply dropped and left to put the pieces of their life back together.

Living as a sociopath gives you an unusual power over others, you are able to see the world without emotions, this allows you plenty of opportunity to plan and scheme over the best way to achieve your aims;

where emotions and fear of hurting other people will stop most people from doing something you will not falter. It is this skill that can make you a great leader, although not necessarily a nice one.

Every opportunity to meet people will be embraced, not because of the need to make a connection with others but because it provides another opportunity to exert your power over others. It also gives you the chance to explore and learn more about personalities; this will help you to understand the human psyche a little better than you already do.

Of course, the lack of guilt and the ability to charm and flatter people does not mean that you will become a manipulative danger to society. There are many sociopaths who exist making all the right sounds and signs whilst holding down a good job and simply watching people. If you are one of these you may always feel like you are looking through a one way mirror; watching people and analysing them without them being able to see what you are doing. You may use your ability to manipulate people to help you obtain what you need, but not be dependent on controlling them long term. Instead of using a person to assist you and provide you with a feeling of power, you are more likely to see everyone as a part of your game. Each person has a role to play in supporting you.

In many ways a sociopath can actually be likened to a major celebrity or world leader; as long as they are popular then people will put up with a huge range of issues; believing they are for the greater good. Perhaps the real question should be, can a sociopath live a normal life and still feel happy and fulfilled?

Chapter 8: How To Deal With Sociopaths

Knowing the general nature of sociopathic individuals, it is very easy to draw on one basic conclusion: sociopaths are a threat. Indeed, even when not all of them are out to kill other people, having a sociopath in your life, be it a friend, a co-worker, a boss, a business partner, a neighbor, a spouse, a romantic partner or a family member, could leave your past, your present, and even your future, with a trail of emotional and psychological wounds and scars.

Before your life could be damaged by the abuse of a sociopath, or before any more harm could be inflicted, it is very important to be able to find a means of protecting yourself before your entire life is totally ruined by the consequences of the sociopath's actions.

Here are some ways on how you can effectively deal with sociopaths in your everyday life and consequently make your way towards healing from their abuse:

Be knowledgeable about the different aspects of sociopathy.

As they would say, "Knowledge is power". This saying definitely rings true as well in your undertaking of successfully dealing with sociopaths in your daily life. Knowing the nature of the condition and its various symptoms and manifestations will allow you to significantly know what to look out for in the individuals you get to mingle with daily.

This awareness will give you the advantage of recognizing who the sociopaths in your life are, if there are any, and consequently, this will allow you to take the next and necessary steps on how you can deal with them.

Avoid the sociopath. And if possible, keep him or her entirely out of your life.

Once you have recognized and made certain that a person in your life is a sociopath, the best and most effective way to protect yourself from the threat of having your life ruined by that person is to avoid them and to keep them out of your life if possible.

Sociopathic individuals are never easy to deal with and the best option that might be best is to totally cut him or her out of your life. Refuse any kind of contact or any form of communication. This may not be easy and in fact, it may even hurt a lot deep inside. But this is the only way to effectively break free from the negative influence of the sociopath.

However, this may not be a workable option for everybody. Especially if the sociopath is a family member, taking them out of your life completely may not be possible. In these cases, just strive to come as close as you can to avoiding them. Or at the very least, learn other effective ways on how to handle their being a part of your life.

Do not join in the sociopath's game.

Despite the threats that they may carry, it cannot be denied that most sociopaths will tend to spark interest or intrigue within you. Some may also tend to easily get onto your nerves. But no matter how tempted you are, always make it a point not to join the game they're playing.

Do not compete with them, do not fall into the traps of their seduction, and do not try to outsmart them, or even have banter with them. Doing so will only give them a space in your life. Remember your goal:

avoid the sociopath at all cost. Keep this in mind at all times and never allow yourself to be distracted from this very essential purpose.

Do not give the sociopath second chances.

It is the nature of humans to have the longing to grant forgiveness and for most people, it is considered to be the right way of living. However, this may not be true when it comes to dealing with sociopaths. In fact, forgiving a sociopath for the damage they have done in your life is considered to be a huge mistake.

Sociopaths are very well aware of our nature to forgive. And unfortunately, no matter how good your intention is, sociopaths will just see this as a weakness and will tend to exploit it. They know that you need to forgive and they will use this against you so they can continue with the cycle of their abuse.

Generally, second chances are only for individuals with a conscience and for those who are genuinely willing to change for the better. But to forgive sociopaths is like opening a door for them to enter your life once again. And this is the best opportunity for them to continue hurting and abusing you.

Manage your emotions well, most especially around the sociopath.

The sociopath will try to use your weaknesses to prey on you. They may be very good in getting on your nerves and in getting into certain topics which may be pretty sensitive for you. But despite all these though, try to hold your ground at all cost. If you are not able to do so, it will only show them that you are weak enough and this will make you more prone to their manipulation.

Even when you are fuming deep inside, try hard to resist the temptation to get into an argument or a dispute with the sociopath. Breathe and just stay calm and casual no matter what they do or say. Do not give them the satisfaction of successfully obtaining the reaction they're trying to get out of you. Always keep your emotions in check no matter what.

Never share any personal information.

Never ever share any personal information to the sociopath. Whether it is about your family and friends, career and business, finances, dreams, or the things that make you happy or sad, do not give the sociopath the liberty or the chance to know about such important matters.

Any information you give them may be used against you. Thus, if you ever get into a conversation with a sociopath, stay on neutral topics and never on important and sensitive matters that may easily be used to manipulate your emotions.

Do not make accusations

Sociopaths never take accusations well. They tend to avoid getting into the spotlight often by smugly shrugging off incriminating claims made against them. They also generally respond aggressively to such damning accusations. Instead of proving the accuser wrong, or facing allegations, the sociopath often even use the accusations as ammunition for his or her mind games. Let us say for example that you have been foolish enough to make an accusation towards a sociopath. To divert attention from them, the sociopath reverses the situation and blames everything back to you, claiming that everything is all your fault, even citing evidences that back the sociopath's misleading assertion. Even if the sociopath is guilty in this situation, his or her mind games are powerful enough to make you feel uneasy and unsure of yourself and the situation. To avoid this in the first place, avoid making any kind of accusations toward the sociopath, no matter how true and positive you think you are. Instead of the sociopath being the victim, in the end, you could be the one getting the worst of the situation.

Avoid power plays with sociopaths

Sociopaths never react well to showcases of imposing influences meant to take control of them or rule over them. Power plays with sociopaths often lead to do more harm than good. They like to be more in control of people than be controlled of people. A sociopath will only see power plays, ultimatums, or such authoritative pressures as one of two things: threat or mind game. When the sociopath sees power plays as a threat, he or she neutralizes the threat by preying on the person doing the power play. On the other hand, when he or she sees the power play as a mind game, the sociopath engages and plays with the minds of the people in authority until a power takeover happens.

Never discuss morality

Sociopaths generally have a low sense of morality in the sense that they usually do not believe in anything morally right or morally wrong. For them, there only is something that is more powerful and something that is less powerful. They do not see moral goodness dictated by emotions or human conscience. They only value what is realistically and logically grounded upon observable phenomenon. Sociopaths will only see discussions about morality as an opportunity to know someone's emotional and moral weaknesses.

Know your weakness

Have a personal reflection and meditation about your own weaknesses. You should know which areas of your life or personality could be your vulnerability to sociopaths. When sociopaths pick their targets and succeed in their mischievous work, it is often because they know a lot about their victims that their victims do not even know about themselves. Sociopaths take notes and build profiles. If you are familiar with your own frailties and weaknesses, then you will know which areas of your life to guard more closely. Also, when a sociopath is trying to take advantage of your weaknesses, you will be aware of it when you already have deeper prior knowledge of things about yourself.

Get professional help

Of course, one of the best ways to deal with sociopaths is to get help from professional therapists who specializes in these kinds of situations. An expert will be able to help you identify the steps and manipulations being done to you by the sociopaths in your life. Getting professional help also minimizes the control of the sociopath over you. Having someone by your side (the professional therapist) will also help restore and alleviate the damages caused by the sociopath to your entire being.

Chapter 9: Living With A Personality Disorder

Anyone who has a personality disorder can find it difficult to complete everyday tasks and may often struggle to contemplate any kind of future. Seeking professional help and taking one day at a time will help dramatically with this, however, there are a number of other techniques and practices which it is important to adopt to ensure a sufferer makes the most of every day and learns to live with a personality disorder:

Stress

Stress is one of the leading causes of a huge range of chronic conditions, including heart attacks and strokes. It is also very detrimental to those with a personality disorder. Stress will place them under additional pressure and make it more likely that they will succumb to the demands of their condition instead of maintaining the therapist's advice.

It is, therefore, essential to devise a daily de-stress plan and stick to it. This may simply be a relaxing bath, walking the dog or even meditation. Whatever the preferred technique, ensuring the levels of stress are kept as low as possible will help anyone to control their extreme reactions.

Yoga

Yoga, or some other similar exercise, allows the opportunity to unwind and refocus the mind. It can also provide an opportunity to escape and allow sufferers to blow off steam in the safety of their own thoughts and mind.

Practicing yoga every day can help to focus the mind and ensure a sufferer can provide their full attention to the tasks which need dealing with on a daily basis. It is therapeutic and not strenuous; this is essential to ensure the mind and body remain calm and ready for the day ahead.

Exercise

A small amount of exercise every day will ensure someone with a personality disorder is in the best possible physical condition. This is essential to build self-worth and confidence in every situation. Feeling good about themselves will help a sufferer to worry less about what others are thinking and doing and focus more on what they should be doing.

Exercising also releases endorphins which make anyone feel good; this can be a natural benefit for anyone struggling with depression and negative emotions. Perhaps the greatest thing about exercise is the ability to do it anywhere; at home, on the street or in the gym. It can be done alone or with others; depending upon your personal preference.

Sleep

The importance of sleep is often underestimated. Sleep allows the brain a chance to relax, process the events of the day and file away useful information. It also allows the body to recuperate and recover, ready to face another day.

Research has shown that insufficient sleep can contribute to negative emotions and an inability to concentrate properly. It has also been linked with an increase in the likelihood of various chronic diseases. Alongside this, sleep, for a personality disorder, is essential to shut the mind down and put the events of one day behind them; ready for a fresh start.

Healthy eating

Taking care of your body and the food and drink you consume is as important as visiting the doctor. A healthy diet will assist anyone suffering from this disorder; they will be in the best physical condition possible and will feel more able to deal with all the events which are thrown at them. It will also boost their confidence levels and counteract negative feelings, such as low self-worth.

A healthy body and mind will assist anyone in having the mental courage to face their disorder and beat it; one step at a time. In addition, there are a whole host of other health benefits; including a decreased chance of sickness, which can lead back to negative thoughts.

Eating healthily is a simple choice to make, it involves thinking about the food consumed and keeping everything in balance; moderation is the key.

Temptation

Many people with personality disorders can find solace in a bottle of alcohol or even some drugs. However, this will not help in the short or long term; in fact a dependency on either of these items is likely to make it much more difficult to focus on their own needs, treatment or even the wider world around them.

The first step towards this is to ensure there is no accessible alcohol or drugs in the house; if it is starting to become an issue it may even be necessary to talk to the local bars and off-licences to ensure they cannot get served.

Professional Help

This topic has been covered within this book, but it cannot be stressed how important it is to seek professional help. A doctor must be the first point of call before a specialist is involved. A therapist will usually be the end result as this person will provide treatment for either as long as it takes or until they feel there is no more benefit in the sessions.

Acknowledging the disorder and obtaining the right help is the most important step in living with the disorder.

Friends & Family

In order to recover from and live with any kind of personality disorder it is essential to build up a good support network. The idea people for this are the family and friends of the person with the disorder. It is best to spend time with them, discussing the issue and what advice has been provided by the doctor or therapist. Once these people know what the sufferer is dealing with they will be able to offer help and support when required.

They will also be the ones that can be turned to on the darker, tough days to ensure the treatment plan is not deviated from and the recovery continues.

Sharing

As the various personality disorders become more talked about and understood there is much more acceptance and information available on the various conditions. People are also now prepared to join online forums and share their experiences. In many cases this can be a beneficial exercise as other people with the same condition can assist with information, guidance and what actions worked for them. Of course, these forums can also be detrimental to some recoveries, particularly the early stages of someone with a histrionic personality disorder who craves the attention.

Learn

Books like this, the internet and even presentations can all provide valuable information on personality disorders in general and specific conditions. They are an invaluable way of learning about a condition; the more that a sufferer or their loved ones know about a specific condition the better able they will be to both assist and combat the disorder.

They say knowledge is power and in this case this is most definitely true. The more everyone knows about these disorders the easier it is to tackle them; both publicly and privately.

Chapter 10: Sociopathic Behavior, Cults And Manson

Sociopaths often attract many followers. Cult leaders and sociopaths often go hand in hand. Cult leaders, like sociopaths often have a great deal of charm and influence over others. Sociopaths are able to encourage other individuals to follow their lead and do what they ask of them which is why many cult leaders are in fact sociopaths. These followers often transform other individuals who may be innocent and sincere into cold-blooded killers. These cult leaders can often be so convincing that they are able to get anything they want and have others do many different things to please them. Individuals often become so fixated on the sociopath that they become mesmerized by this individual. Cult leaders, like sociopaths are masters at manipulating the emotions of others. One commonality between the two is their use of words. Both sociopaths and cult leaders have a way with words, they are able to be charming, convincing and persuasive all at the same time. What's so disturbing about this is that our emotions often affect the way we live our life. If we are insecure, we often show these insecurities to others, if we love something, we will show others how we feel. When someone is manipulating and disturbing our emotions, they can often create unhealthy, insecure person who most likely was a very stable individual beforehand. No one is too strong to be conned or manipulated. There are CEO's, directors of organizations, business owners, and immense amount of other professionals who have been conned. Many of these individuals started off as very stable individuals and allowed themselves to become trusting of other individuals and their actions. An example of this would be someone in a high position at work getting conned by someone they may start to have feelings for. Men and women often prey on those who they feel they can make a significant impact on. Life is nothing more than a game for cult leaders and sociopaths. The game of life entitles the sociopath to be the leader and everyone else is nothing more than a player in this game. Each game player can be moved by the leader in any way the leader or sociopath seems fit.

Keep in mind that these individuals, while yes, they are creating negativity in the world, they have no feelings or emotions about what they're doing and therefore it doesn't affect them. This careless behavior actually draws other individuals to follow their lead. When someone seems to be strong in any situation without any emotion, this is viewed as an attractive behavior. When individuals cry, seem distraught, become upset or show any other type of emotion, this is often viewed as a weak individual. For example, when men cry, they're often said to be weak. That being said, when someone cries or shows emotion, they are not weak individuals, they are real individuals with real feelings. Many cult leaders and sociopaths are often men because it's easier for them to show emotion. It seems more logical and ordinary for a man to hold back from showing emotion as opposed to a woman. That being said, there are definitely a significant amount of women who are also considered sociopaths in the world. Cult leaders, like sociopaths thrive off of dominating others. These individuals want nothing more than to lead a situation. Cult leaders like sociopaths first start off with a charming attitude. They make other individuals think that they're caring, loving and empathetic individuals when in reality, they want nothing more than for you as their victim to do what they say and follow their lead.

Sociopaths are more often than not leaders which make sociopaths and cult leader's one in the same. With cults however, the cult leader is often able to gather groups of individuals and encourage them to follow their lead and obey their rules. Sociopaths are often different in that they often attack a single person or one person at a time rather then preying on individuals. Cult leaders for example, have been known to encourage large groups of people to follow what they say and whatever they want them to do. Throughout history, cults have become an intimidation group formation that has led to many negative and harmful acts. Going back to Charles Manson however, he was able to orchestrate one of the most famous mass murders in history. Manson alone, encouraged his followers to commit multiple murders in the 1960's. This sociopath showed very early signs of sociopathic behaviors. He initially showed signs of wanting to be accepted and when he wasn't, he began to lash out at the world. The intense need for society to accept him although he suffered from psychiatric disorders. Early on, he was incarcerated for smaller crimes such as passing out stolen checks. These crimes put him in jail where he continued to act out. While these petty crimes were small, they were crimes none the less and showed that Manson was on a destructive path. After this, he continued on to organize the famous Hollywood murders.

Manson began living an unconventional lifestyle once released from jail. He became very influenced by music, scientology, and drugs. Manson gathered his first group of followers together based on his love of LSD a hallucinogenic that was very popular in the 1960's. This drug was not only addictive but it made individuals do things they normally would not. Lsd and magic mushrooms became very popular amongst the group Manson had gathered together. This unconventional lifestyle and great love of hardcore drugs set this group aside from others. It was a place to live freely with no restrictions. Eventually, they became known simply as "the family". Initially, he was able to gather around 100 followers. This fairly large group included a group of very young girls who were easily influenced by Manson, drugs and others. These girls were so young, naïve, and impressionable that they actually believed that Manson was in fact Jesus. Considering the fact that many sociopaths actually believe their own lies, it's very likely that Manson in fact believed that he was Jesus and that he could make anything happen that he wanted to happen.

These murders took place on August 9, 1969 at the house of Roman Polanski in

Beverly Hills. For this specific crime, Manson herded together four of his top followers. The group consisted of one man and three woman which showed that while his followers were both male and female, he had more female followers than male followers. Now, this isn't to say that woman are more vulnerable than men, but what it does show is that Manson, being the sociopath that he is, chose to prey upon more women than men, especially young women. He handpicked these individuals and prepared them to kill the "beautiful people" in Beverly Hills. Now, keep in mind that sociopaths are usually desperate for attention, if Manson saw that these famous individuals were receiving attention in Hollywood and in the media, he most likely was jealous of this in some sick and twisted way. Manson most likely chose these individuals to kill because they represented Hollywood, they represented a life that he would never be a part of.

Manson was having trouble fitting into society by itself, he most likely, would have never made it into Hollywood and this angered him. Sociopaths always try and get what they want one way or another. Being that Manson did not get what he wanted, he needed to get revenge on those who did receive in life, what Manson ultimately wanted. This hatred for his non-followers overwhelmed him. For Manson, something had to be done to cause pain to others and this is what encouraged the murders to take place.

The most famous victim that was killed this night was Sharon Tate who happened to be pregnant. This heinous crime, while it was committed by Manson's followers, he orchestrated the entire process. Manson had a plan and he was able to complete this plan and this goal without actually committing any murders in the process. Manson is one of the most well-known sociopath cult leaders because of his ability to get this group to actually kill for him. Manson stood back and watched his plan in action, he watched innocent individuals stabbed and shot to death. He stood back and watched a pregnant woman being stabbed in the stomach and killed. Manson watched as his followers used Tate's blood to write "pig" on the wall. It's bad enough to watch someone commit a murder but to have orchestrated the entire thing and feel absolutely nothing, to feel no remorse shows what a true sociopath Manson was. Manson not only didn't feel any remorse for what took place, but he orchestrated more murders soon after the murder of Sharon Tate and her friends.

With sociopaths, it doesn't matter how big the crime is, how severe the pain is, the sociopath will feel absolutely no remorse or empathy. There are individuals who commit crimes, murder individuals and still feel remorse and feel as though they wish they wouldn't have done what they did. With sociopaths, there is absolutely no feeling involved in this. This lack of feeling and emotion is what drives sociopaths to encourage others to follow him. If the sociopath doesn't care what he does and how he hurts other individuals, there is absolutely no hope that he will worry about other individuals hurting someone else as well. With cult leaders and sociopaths, they want others to believe what they believe in, they want others to follow their lead and look at them as though they rule the world. This is exactly how Manson's followers looked up to him. Manson was able to be so convincing to his followers that they viewed him as their savior. They viewed Manson as a god and they knew that they needed to do anything they could to please him even if that meant killing others and taking their lives. Manson, among other sociopaths and cult leaders still sits in jail. In fact, he recently married a young woman which shows that his sociopathic charm still works. The fact that Manson was able to convince someone, who is not in jail, to marry him, shows the power and charm that he still holds. Manson, the face of pure evil, convinced yet another woman to fall in love with him and give her life to him. Sociopaths will always have this hold over others. Regardless of the situation they're in, whether they're in jail, talking to someone over the internet or at a bar somewhere, they're able to be so convincing that they can literally make certain individuals do anything for them. Sociopaths can be anyone from the scary, homeless looking man walking down the street, to the handsome man you met at the grocery store. Sociopaths can be children, they can be the beautiful new employee that your company hired. Sociopaths are unfortunately, everywhere in the world. Do not let these individuals scam you. If something seems off, and if it doesn't match up, look into this. Do not let someone make you believe that they're god, that they're the best thing that's happened to the world today. Stand your ground and always stay on the lookout for these individuals. Be strong in your views and who you are as an individual. Sociopaths and cult leaders prey on the weak, no matter what your insecurities are, be strong when you are communicating with others, you never know when someone is in tune with your insecurities and when someone is trying to convince you that they're something they're not. If someone seems too good to be true, they probably are. Do not be overly cautious about making new friends, but don't hand over a $500 loan to a friend you met last week either. Like anything else in life, be cautious with your relationships and understand that there are both good and bad people in the world. Weed out the sociopaths and let honest individuals into your life.

Chapter 11: Are You Experiencing Antisocial Personality Disorder

You now have a great deal of information from the definition of antisocial personality disorder to how psychologists break it down into psychopathy and sociopathy. If you feel you may have a problem, it is not wise to diagnose yourself. Most individuals who try to self-diagnose misread the characteristics and severity of their actual problem.

Is it possible that you could be experiencing some characteristics of antisocial personality disorder, psychopathy, or sociopathy? Yes, there may be times when you feel little remorse or guilt in a situation or are easy to anger. The difference between normal instances of such feelings and those with the disorder is a pervasive, steady consistency in showing these characteristics.

It must also be mentioned that someone who is antisocial does not have to fit the category of antisocial personality disorder. There are other behavioral disorders as well as social disorders that can bring about antisocial behaviors. Someone who does not socialize often or care to leave the house may have a social anxiety disorder that causes panic attacks and fear to set in. This is totally different in terms of a diagnosis than an antisocial personality disorder like sociopathy or psychopathy.

If you feel you have a problem or are experiencing some of the characteristics as outlined by Hare and Cleckley, then you should seek a clinical diagnosis. You may have a very mild disorder, which allows you to recognize there is an issue and seek help for it. Most individuals with a severe disorder do not have the desire to discover the why of their behavior. This goes back to the lack of remorse, empathy, guilt, and other societal viewed norms. Instead of asking why or caring about why individuals with severe disorders tend to just act as suits them best.

It is another reason that self-diagnosing can lead you to the wrong conclusion. It is better to leave the experts to their job. If you do feel there is an issue, start off by getting help and a full physical. Tumors and other illnesses can affect how the brain functions. A good example of this is thyroid disorder. Thyroid disorder is known for causing depression, dementia like symptoms, and extreme anger. An individual with social anxiety issues can become more anxious and fearful when their thyroid hormones are not regulated properly. From the example you can see that there may be a medical answer to the feelings, thoughts, or lack of emotions you are feeling right now. It also clearly indicates the pitfalls that can occur should you try to diagnose issues on your own.

It may be necessary to have someone in your life tell you that you need help and be appointed as the person that makes sure you receive it. It is a good idea for anyone whether they feel there is an issue or not to already have medical and financial power of attorney documents in place. In this way if there are behavioral issues you might get the help you need earlier.

Chapter 12: Destructive Behaviour

When I joined the Freedom Programme with my local Domestic Abuse support group, one of the most memorable sessions was that one where they asked us if our partner had ever burnt our breakfast throughout the years together.

Bizarre question, right?

But what was even more bizarre was that every single one of us answered in turns, 'Ever? How about every time?', 'He put things in the food that I'm allergic to, without a fail', 'When had I ever have sugar in my tea in all the years we were together??'

All sorts of very bizarre, some quite worrying, anecdotes kept on coming, and we naturally went on a wider range of other weird stuff going on in the household like, 'I had to give up buying white clothes because he would ruin them every single time I asked him to put a washing', 'How is it possible to make fluff hoovering?', 'My socks kept on disappearing', ...

But the real point of the question was to realise that not only we didn't imagine it because this was happening to others too, it was also about realising that this **didn't happen just once**, that it was a **recurrent** unusual thing that kept on happening **throughout the years**. Unusual, because no normal person would make a mistake like that over and over and over again: Normal people learn. And that was the real red flag.

It turns out that a common denominator for perpetrators is to purposely ruin and boycott things that they have been asked for. The reason behind (hidden agenda again) is that they want to discourage you from asking, because they want you to give up and do it yourself, for both of you.

This is not a trait of normal people. Normal people make mistakes, and learn.

Abusers persist in not learning from their "mistakes", and if you continue asking them to do the tasks, they will perceive it as nagging, and they might even take the game up a notch, starting to do more harmful things.

'The first time that my partner added to the meal something I had an intolerance to, I fell for the apologies.

'As it continued happening, I got increasingly annoyed. It wasn't life threatening, but awfully uncomfortable, and sometimes very painful.

'After two years, I couldn't tell whether he was punishing me for something, or he was mentally challenged.'

This type of behaviour is not a mistake, it follows a pattern.

'I think the weirdest one that he ever did was when after the breakup he came back from a trip and brought me a little cake of raisins at work, very randomly.

'I can't stand raisins, I have never liked them, I'm not raisin intolerant but if I find raisins in my pudding I do send it back to the kitchen, and he was well aware of it.

'So there I was, at work, with a raisin cake on my hands, wondering if he was having a laugh or completely demented, while my colleagues praised his "come back" effort.

'And then he called to ask if I had liked his gesture.'

Understand that this is not normal behaviour.

Normal would have been not bringing anything, since he never did while they were together. Or doing it in private, and not as a public display to gain praise from strangers. Or not bringing her something he knew she hated. Or not calling her to ask her how she liked being given things she hated.

The reality of that situation was that he didn't need to do any of those things. Not one of them. He was aiming to provoke, and that was the real reason behind.

Creating an issue in order to trigger a conflict

Have you ever lived with someone who creates problems where there shouldn't be? It is genuinely exhausting.

You spend your waking hours rearranging appointments, dealing with angry people about "misunderstandings", paying extra fees, bending back and for to make your daily plans accommodate the unexpected, investing all your energy in solving the problems this person lands on you, and being blamed for most or the whole of it when you wouldn't even think of provoking such situations in which you have been involved by the other person in the first place.

In other words: You end up fixing what your partner breaks, for living, but without pay.

And yes, as we mentioned in Chapter 3 (The Importance of Accountability), it becomes a mess. You end up losing yourself because you spend so much time fixing what the other person breaks, that you simply have no time left for you.

It is definitely not normal behaviour, it is odd and destructive. Nobody wants to be involved in difficult situations that could have been avoided. At least no normal person would.

Beware of Patterns

The thing about destructive behaviour is that:

- If there isn't a pattern, you have nothing to worry about. It won't repeat itself, naturally.

- If there is a pattern, that's bad. It's not random, someone has an agenda.

For instance, do you have a random argument with your partner every time you want to go out?

Or does something involving your partner always come up that forces you to cancel the going out, and after a while you just give up trying?

Think about when was the last time that this was not the case, that you could be excited about going out, and actually do it, and not fear the consequences.

Think about when was the last time that you had fun together with your partner, without spoilers or a bad aftertaste.

Think about how much you trust your partner to do things without having to argue about it.

Think about how much you are appreciated regularly.

And criticised?

Agendas have a purpose, generally a destructive one, and with a purpose comes a pattern.

If you are being victim of one, you need to consider that no one who truly loves you would use patterns to manipulate you for any purpose. Because that would be wrong, and harmful.

Projecting Negativity

Destructive behaviour is also about spoiling life for you.

This includes making you feel like you never do anything worth praising. Burying you in responsibilities that should have been shared. Putting so much on you that you neither have the time nor the energy to do something for yourself. Making it impossible for you to have any "me" time. Dismissing your achievements, and putting you down at any opportunity...

In normal circumstances, this shouldn't really happen in the relationship. If it is happening, you need to reconsider the situation, bearing in mind that it is destructive behaviour, that there is a pattern, and that it is not an expression of love.

Destructive behaviour is an expression of hatred.

Whatever it is the reason for this expression to take place, it is not right. It is not acceptable.

This is not how relationships are supposed to be, it is not reasonable to put you through it, but most importantly, you do not have to take it.

Don't.

Chapter 13: Repair Your Relationship:

Necessary Steps to Regain Control and Build a Healthy Relationship

People never plan to be in abusive relationships. As a matter of fact, most never realize that they are in an abusive relationship until it's already too late. People who have never been victims of abusive and controlling partners will always have a difficult time understanding how someone can get abused and not realize that. If you are amongst these people, be grateful and do not be judgmental. Controlling and abusive partners will never show their true colors on the first dates. As discussed in previous chapters, they are very affectionate during the embryonic stages of a relationship.

This makes the other person rush and make commitments thinking they have found "Mr. or Mrs. Right".

Once you realize you are, in fact, romantically involved with a toxic partner, follow these strategies to regain control.

Recognize the signs.

The first and foremost step is to recognize and accept that you are in a relationship that is abusive. Living in denial is always catastrophic. You may be feeling that your partner is just an overbearing jerk and that he or she is not that bad. It's until you accept that your partner is abusive that you can have better chances of regaining control in such a relationship. Having discussed different types of abuse in the previous chapter, it should be easy for you to realize that your partner is abusing you emotionally, verbally, sexually or physically. Be honest with yourself, don't deny that you are being abused.

Recognizing this abuse is the first step to fighting it, keeping in mind that you just can't allow it to continue.

Set limits on your partner's emotional outbursts and criticism.

Make sure that your partner is aware that you are always open to hear their concerns. Make sure that they know how their actions affect you as a person. Let them know that you are no longer comfortable to engage in conversations that attack your personality. If you are a woman, the man that is abusing you may be the only man in the world that you love with all your heart, but this does not mean that you should allow him to make you feel like you are in prison. Let him know that you can even quit the relationship if that will give you peace.

Deal with negative criticism in a positive way.

In most cases, victims of abuse react to their partner's actions or words without thinking of their beliefs first. Listen to your partner's criticism, offensive words and intimidation and try to react to them positively. For example, criticism on the part of your earnings should stimulate you to work harder or in a more innovative way to further your career, instead of having self-pity. This will turn the tables as soon as your partner recognizes that you are actually improving in the aspects that they criticize you on.

Consider your partner's concerns.

What are you willing to offer your partner? Ensure that whatever you want to do for them will be beneficial to both of you. Do not agree to do anything in desperation in order to save your relationship, especially if deep down in your heart you are aware that it is not right for you.

Don't overreact.

Avoid heated arguments with your partner over an abusive behavior at all costs. Arguments will only add an insult to the injury. Instead, do your best not to take things personally and let it go. Practice self-control and above all, respect yourself.

Be honest with yourself first before being honest with your partner.

Consider your needs, goals and values. Ensure that any decision that you make is for your own benefit first. Let your partner know your boundaries; what you can and cannot do for them. Do not be intimidated in whatever you want to do. Whenever you disagree, be clear by having a powerful "No". Be clear that whenever you say "no" they have no option, but to respect your decision. If they cannot respect your decision, it's best for both of you to go separate ways.

Secretly save money.

If your abusive partner is controlling the finances, set up a secret account. If you can't set a secret account, look for a place that is far away from the house and save your own money. For example, you can use your office locker. You can also give your money to a friend whom you trust to keep your money on your behalf. Another alternative place where you can safely keep your money is inside a safe deposit box. Just in case you receive your paychecks through direct deposits, make sure that some of that cash is transferred to a different account.

Get help.

The biggest mistake that most people, especially women, do is staying in abusive relationships because they always feel embarrassed to tell their family members and friends what's really going on. If they have partners who behave like "Mr. or

Mrs. Perfect" when they are in public, they may have a feeling that nobody will believe what they say. In this case, you should also look for help through online resources. You must not allow yourself to undergo this kind of suffering alone.

Get your power back.

The easiest way of doing this is walking away from the relationship if the situation is beyond repair. This will enable to make progress not from a position of weakness, but from a position of strength.

Find people who celebrate who you are.

Look for ways that will assist you in rediscovering yourself. Connect and engage with people who will unconditionally love you and support you irrespective of your shortcomings. It's only you who can make a decision whether to live with your toxic partner or not. You must be in a relationship that supports your growth and not a relationship that puts you down. You have a right to be in a loving relationship; you must, therefore, love yourself. It's always the main step towards regaining control when you are in a relationship with an abusive partner.

Having said that, not all dysfunctional relationships are doomed. It is possible for abusers in a relationship to change if they admit what they have done, stop the blame game and make the necessary amends. This will lead to a healthy relationship with is characterized by love, care and understanding. A healthy relationship involves two people, connected on a deep psychological level. At the same time, each partner is responsible for their own happiness. Together, they make their happiness complete. A partner does not put boundaries on the life of their loved one. Overall, everyone lives life at their own pace.

A healthy relationship is one where each partner recognizes and appreciates the needs of the other. Each partner in a relationship demands something different from the other person. This explains why in most cases, getting the right partner is easier said than done. Women need to respect their men unconditionally. If you are able to give your man unconditional respect, he will be the happiest man in the world. He will be satisfied and content. On the other hand, women need unconditional love from the men in their lives. If you love your woman truly and unconditionally, she will feel as if she owns the world. This way, there is mutual understanding and benefit. In a healthy relationship, every partner works towards its success. Relationships are said to be like a football match, where everybody plays their part to avoid defeat. You have to work hard to ensure that your love life is successful, but you should not give all your life to your partner.

All relationships are as unique as the people in them. This means that there is no exact recipe for happiness. There is no exact number of laughs; there are no exact types of romance. A relationship grows and evolves with the people that make them. That being said, there are certain characteristics of a healthy relationship. These are constant. Keep in mind that people do argue and no one is perfect. A healthy relationship does not mean there are no conflicts within it. Rather, it is about the way two people relate to each other.

There is not one thing that makes a couple work. It is a combination of factors and the way two people unite that creates a good, healthy relationship. The factors, or characteristics, that make a couple work are important. Stress creates conflict and people make mistakes. It is the way a couple deals with problems that dictate the type of relationship they have. Factors such as trust, respect, and understanding are all a part of this. In fact, these following factors should be a set goal for all couples to reach. Above all else, love and the wish to make a relationship great is what makes relationships last.

Respect.

Many psychologists will agree that respect is vital for both the individual and the couple as a whole. In a relationship, it is important that the respect is mutual. Respect is shown in many ways. The wishes and needs of both partners are important. This means that both partners' opinions carry equal weight. In spite of disagreements, they should be able to listen and appreciate what the other is saying. It is also important not to lose the individuals within the relationships. Excessive jealousy and control can force a person to conform to the rules that they don't agree with. When their privacy and character are invaded, the relationship itself suffers. Respecting each other for who they both are and allowing each other privacy is key. Within healthy relationships, both partners appreciate each other's families, obligations and views.

Trust and Honesty.

Trust and honesty go hand in hand. Without one, the other is impossible. In other words, if a person does not trust their partner, they will not be able to be honest. A couple should be honest about many issues. These issues include the way a person feels, thinks, behaves and so on. Yet this can be complicated. This happens if either or both of them experienced rejection when being honest in the past. This is a process. Couples spend their whole lives trusting and being honest. Despite the fact that people make mistakes, a strong couple is one which can forgive and move forward. This, of course, must be mutual and fair. If one is always forgiving while the other is constantly letting them down, then this is not a healthy relationship.

Communication.

For any relationship to function, good communication skills are needed. Every couple converses in their own way. Some people are more talkative while others are quiet. This is irrelevant. What is relevant is that they understand each other. Within a healthy couple, both partners listen, as well as talk. Even when arguing, they are able to do so with a positive tone. For example, they may disagree about who spent more money, but they do not judge or blame each other. They also do not dismiss or degrade the person they love. An argument in a healthy relationship is more a debate than a fight. They also take the time to explain their thoughts and emotions.

Compromise and boundaries.

It is well known that compromise is a big part of any committed relationship. As with every other aspect mentioned this must be mutual. Any compromise made must not be too great a sacrifice. A loving partner would never ask for this. Instead, the compromise would be one that both partners can live with. It is also fair. If one partner cannot compromise, he or she is not met with aggression. In a healthy relationship, partners to do not threaten each other to get what they want. Throughout the healthy relationship, both partners compromise respectively. This can be something small, like what restaurant to eat at. It can also be something more important, like who pursues their career first. That being said, there have to be boundaries. Both partners should be able to keep all the things they find important. In a thriving relationship, no one is forced to do anything, and both sides have the right to choose.

Affection, intimacy and friendship.

These three factors complement each other in a healthy relationship. Begin with friendship. There is a difference between a relationship and a friendship. However, make your partner your greatest friend. Some people just rush to the romantic side of a relationship, forgetting the simple things that make a relationship last. You cannot climb a tree from the top. For this reason, it is important to ensure that you are great friends first, so that this friendship can grow into a healthy and loving relationship.

Affection is shown through kind words and compliments. It is also shown through non-sexual touch. This refers to holding hands, hugging and gentle kissing. This affection, in turn, creates a strong intimacy. People, in general, have different sexual preferences. A healthy relationship does not mean that the couple makes love on a daily basis. It also does not exclude this as a possibility. What it does mean is that both partners enjoy this intimacy. This deep bond exists due to the friendship that is present. This friendship is like no other, and it is vital. A healthy relationship means that both partners enjoy each other's company. They have fun, they confide in each other, and they keep each other's secrets. It is, in fact, the connection that makes a healthy relationship possible.

Understanding and support.

Understand the needs of your partner. Your partner's needs are different from yours. Understand and appreciate these needs and do your best to satisfy the ones you can.

Self-love and self-respect.

Love yourself first. You need to love yourself first before loving your partner. It is okay to be selfish sometimes in a relationship. Find your happiness from within. The worst mistake you can make in a relationship is to rely on your partner to be happy in life. You will always find yourself unhappy, because he or she may not give you all the happiness you may need.

Positive and realistic attitude.

Take it easy. There is nothing that is so serious in this life. Also, do not expect too much from your partner.

For a relationship to exist, the couple must love each other. In some cases, unfortunately, people exist together but are not committed. It is this commitment that defines a relationship. All loving couples should strive to be as healthy and happy as possible. A healthy relationship is one which gets better in time, with growing respect, communication and the ability to listen, honesty, trust and friendship. All these things are possible to be achieved with time and they will create a beautiful history. A strong couple looks at this history with joy, not regret.

For any couple to be healthy, both partners need to work on this. This work, on its own, is the embodiment of a healthy relationship. This mutual wish to make each other better and be proud of each other is what helps couples to be happy. In summary, it is possible for people to stop their abusiveness, regain control and build a healthy and fulfilling relationship. However, this takes discipline, understanding and hard work.

Chapter 14: Treatment For Psychopaths And Sociopaths

APD is usually misunderstood by both professionals and laymen in relation to the psychopath and sociopath. This makes treatment difficult. Another reason treatment becomes difficult is because many patients never seek help due to the stigma attached to the conditions. While some people hope there is medicine to treat sociopaths and psychopaths, there is none. In fact, there is no evidence of treating patients using medications. Therefore, the only option viable is psychotherapy.

In many cases, patients are referred for therapy sessions by a court of law. This becomes tricky as the patients will by then be serving prison terms and cannot get the chance to relate with people under normal circumstances. In confined settings, achieving desired results is difficult. Another hitch is the inability of patients to open up. Once a therapist tries to talk about their feelings, the sociopath and psychopath become mute. They believe their secrets at deceit may be discovered.

Some therapists try to use threats to make patients comply. This hardly ever works. If a clinician threatens to report the patient to the authorities for non-compliance, they mostly hide under their cocoons and remain silent or go on the offensive. In brief, these two disorders have very limited treatment. A clinician may make headways only if the patient trusts them, which is often very rare. All the same, when they open up, they are capable of obtaining help, albeit little.

The sociopaths and psychopaths are as many as can be, though a number of people do not realize it. They are friends, relatives, workmates, neighbors, church members and even many more. When one realizes they are in the company of the two, they must seek help as soon as they can. This way, they may save themselves a lot of trouble.

Chapter 15: Sociopaths And Psychopaths Among Children

No medical or clinical diagnosis can be made before the age of 18. As such, terming a child as a psychopath or sociopath may not be appropriate. Having said that, there are some signs of sociopathy and psychopathy which become evident from childhood itself. Growing up pangs are numerous and isolating a particular trait becomes difficult. Children show signs of ADHD, depression, aggression, withdrawal from normal activities and so on. However there are some specific traits in children which may cause concern to parents.

George was a happy child and liked by everyone. The only problem which his parents noticed was his liking for poking their dog Kelly with a fork. By the time George was eight, Kelly had been burnt with a hot iron several times. Kelly used to whimper in fear and dread whenever she saw George. He loved to catch butterflies in the garden, remove their wings and watched them die. Though the parents tried to stop him from undertaking such sadistic activities, George continued without paying any attention. The parents simply could not understand the behavior of their child. There were complaints from school that George was routinely flouting rules and was a bully. When caught, he used to outright refuse to accept that he was wrong. He was indifferent to the pain which he inflicted on others.

Another trait which emerged was that George was a compulsive liar. His parents suspected that he stole money from them. Their suspicion was confirmed when they found a roll of cash stashed away in his cupboard carefully hidden from sight. Why would a child steal? George was not old enough to go out and spend the money. George never showed guilt or remorse even if his lie was caught.

His parents decided to take him for counseling finally, when George was ten. The diagnosis came as a blow and the parents were aghast to know that George was suffering from a serious illness. Though no medical condition can be medically ascertained before the age of 18, the prognosis was bleak. George was in all probability, suffering from psychopathy.

The story of George is not unique. Psychopaths and sociopaths start showing signs of deviant behavior from an early stage in life. Parents should carefully monitor their children for the above signs and seek help as early as possible. It is unfortunate that this particular psychological condition is not curable.

However, you can stop your child from committing a serious crime or misdemeanor. There have been instances when children with psychopathic tendencies have murdered or maimed other children. Children suffering from psychopathy do not show any remorse. They do not display normal emotions. Parents of such children ignore the signs of psychopathy in their children till they land in trouble involving the police and law. Paradoxically, many psychopaths get away with all their fiendish activities and reach the top of their chosen profession. It is possible that excessive aggression can be mistaken for psychopathy. This kind of behavior still needs counselling and behavior therapy.

Chapter 16: Objectifying Women as Sociopaths

Media attention has been focusing on the misogynistic objectification and business corruption. These recently examined phenomena will likely reveal narcissistic sociopaths as their centers.

Narcissistic sociopaths see women (certainly all people) as somethings and not someones. They will also bilk the working class and poor with their hard-earned and urgently needed cash.

Narcissists have a tendency to be impulsive, need for affection and show a pattern of grandiosity in their dreams or conduct. Sociopaths, or those with a diagnosed antisocial personality disorder, have a pattern of disrespect for and offense to the rights of others. They also lack remorse even though they lie, cheat, steal, and are often referred to as sociopaths.

Although narcissism is often a single personality disorder within an individual, it's not uncommon for sociopathy and narcissism to co-occur within that individual.

A narcissistic sociopath will see little distinction between cars, televisions, couches and fire hydrants. All of them are just objects to be used for entertainment or personal gain. This is why objectification can be considered a key feature in this type of psychopathology.

It's not the fault of the NS, however! They see themselves as extraordinary and claim that the law and proper social conduct do not apply to them. This is because they lack one essential attribute that defines people (and most likely other advanced mammals). Namely, empathy. Empathy is the ability to place oneself in another's shoes and attempt to understand their feelings, thoughts, and dignity. This is to care for someone other than yourself.

NSs lack empathy because they don't have the brain physiology or neurological structures required to feel empathy. They lack the brain devices necessary to care for others.

Color loss of sight is one example. The optical and neurological procedures required to see the entire spectrum of color in visible wavelength length are not available to color blind people. They are not blind, but they can't see certain colors or hues. Narcissistic sociopaths, on the other hand, don't have the ability to experience all of the human emotions that are characteristic of mentally healthy people. They don't seem to have the tools to understand.

However, this doesn't excuse or give them the right to be bad people. This just clarifies their inability to grasp the concept. They don't understand why you don't lie, cheat or take, manipulate, betray, and abuse others. You can always get another one if you damage your TV, wreck your car, or destroy your couch. NSs don't see any distinction between humans and things, so people are also quickly disposable and replaceable. A NS emotionally doesn't see any difference between a sexy inflatable and a human being. They are just objects or things to be used for him/her.

However, merely pointing out antisocial behavior does not excuse it.

Why is it that some sociopaths are successful while others are not? It often comes down to intelligence and impulse control. The "successful" sociopaths are able to exercise restraint and control their spontaneity, as well as compensate for their emotional gaps with their intellect.

Most NSs who are unsuccessful have poor impulse control. They also likely don't intellectually compensate for their psychological deficiencies, which can lead to them being ostracized and even in prison.

My belief is that "successful NSs" tend to gravitate towards jobs such as medicine, law, and business. Although I know that this is a broad generalization and one that I can't back up with controlled research, it makes sense that those courses attract NSs. It also makes sense that NSs could lack empathy in these settings which could lead to them being more adaptive, thus leading to success.

The million-dollar question that I get is, "How do you deal NS?" My usual answer is to "Keep as far as possible away from narcissistic sociopaths!" It is enough to avoid manipulative people, even those without conscience.

Conclusion

Be mindful of those people you so choose to call your friends. Psychotic breaks or episodes are just around the corner for most of us. Studies show that 85% of people will develop a mental illness at some point in their lives. Not every psychopath will become a murderer or serial killer despite what many believe. Experts think about 40% of people are psychopathic. This loss of empathy may just be the next step in our evolution as a species.

Empathy and feelings could be considered an issue for the success of future generations. It is up for debate as to whether being "good" benefits us in life. "Bad" can be used against the "good" people and could be seen as a weakness. Survival of the fittest is an old-world theory. Now, because of medical advances, healthy food options, the internet and knowledge at our fingertips, health inspectors, USDA food administrations, and so more; it is no wonder people are living longer.

Mental illness can manifest itself in many ways. The criminally insane are not justified as to what they do that is morally and ethically wrong according to society and the safety of everyone else. There is no justifying killing or any action or behavior that cause trauma or harm to anyone else.

According to the experts, the criminally insane and other disordered personalities were predisposed to their conditions. No one's brain wiring is set in stone; however, some people meet certain criteria that make them more vulnerable than other people to become a psychopath, sociopath, or disordered personality.

Some people have the constitution to endure and become successful in whatever they take on in life. Conversely, some people are abused to the point that they cannot be repaired or rehabilitated. We will all have our experiences with mental illness one day, whether it is a friend, family, or yourself.